D1092633

TOWARDS WINNING

TOWARDS WINNING

6 STEPS TO TRANSFORM YOUR LIFE

KARUNAKAR B.

JAICO PUBLISHING HOUSE

Ahmedabad Bangalore Bhopal Bhubaneswar Chennai
Delhi Hyderabad Kolkata Lucknow Mumbai

Published by Jaico Publishing House
A-2 Jash Chambers, 7-A Sir Phirozshah Mehta Road
Fort, Mumbai - 400 001
jaicopub@jaicobooks.com
www.jaicobooks.com

© Karunakar B.

TOWARDS WINNING
ISBN 978-93-86867-62-9

First Jaico Impression: 2018

No part of this book may be reproduced or utilized in
any form or by any means, electronic or
mechanical including photocopying, recording or by any
information storage and retrieval system,
without permission in writing from the publishers.

Page design and layout: Inosoft Systems, Delhi

Printed by
Thomson Press (India) Limited

For my son Aditya Vikram;
nieces Pranati, Jyotsna, Anushree & Hithushree;
nephews Prajwal, Shreyes, Vivek & Aayush;
and my students

A man who sees inaction in action
and action in inaction
has understanding among men,
disciplined in all action he performs.

—The *Bhagavad Gita*, Chapter 4, *Shloka* 18
(translated by Barbara Stoler Miller)

CONTENTS

PRELUDE

What is this book about? For whom is this book written and why?

This book narrates the story of Dev, his professional journey and his reflections on management techniques. It explains the use of certain management tools that helped Dev reinvent his career and personal life.

If you are a management professional desiring to make a transition to leadership by enhancing your management skills for high-impact performance, then this book will provide you with compelling insights to do exactly that.

By stepping into Dev's shoes, I am sure that everyone reading this book will get the perfect motivational kick for leading a powerful life. The story will provide answers to a young professional, eager to shape his life and career. Today's young professional is groping his way in a technologically advanced environment and is deluged with lots of options. The challenge is much more in terms of decision-making and making the right choices than from Dev's times in the '80s. But the fundamentals remain the same when it comes to walking with wisdom and taking the correct decision.

For the question "What has changed since then?" the answer

is paradoxical. While quite a few things have changed, some have remained unchanged. For instance, the mode of transport has changed from bullock carts to cars. While at first there were only brick houses, there are now iron and steel high-rises as well. The war strategies have changed. But have we changed as human beings fundamentally? Have we evolved equally? Do we now have less conflicts and better understanding? Is there better teamwork? Has the leadership quotient gone up? Do we have more leaders than yesterday? The book provides a perspective on these questions.

The story will not only help young professionals but also middle-aged and senior working professionals, as I narrate some of the critical choices that Dev had to make at different times and how he made the tryst with destiny as he kept growing from a young to a seasoned professional.

This book is therefore helpful for any person who has embarked on a career. He could be in any profession. This book will surely help you in finding the answer to the question: "What button do I need to press to ignite and transform my life?" For those who have already found the answer, this book will still be worth a read as it will resonate with their findings and confirm their discoveries on winning, and finally making a difference for themselves and others.

The book consists of eight chapters. Each chapter is replete with diagrams, models and pictures to emphasize the management tools that can be used for effective decision-making to win in life.

Chapter 1: Challenges

This chapter addresses the salient point on developing leadership qualities and underscores the importance of challenge, willingness and support. Even if one of them is absent, the desired outcomes or results do not materialize. In other words, successful outcomes or results cannot be achieved without the simultaneous operation of challenge, willingness and support.

Chapter 2: Inner Winner

This chapter deals with the *hows* of becoming an inner winner. To become an inner winner, you need to work on four things (1) Weekly planning (2) Writing your purpose/mission statement and values that guide your decisions (3) Exercising the freedom to choose and developing a winner's mindset (4) The power of taking feedback and using autosuggestions to work on strong points and overcome the weaknesses. This chapter is the first step in transforming your life.

Chapter 3: Outer Winner

This chapter explains the application of the key elements of inner and outer winner. While it is indeed an effort to become an inner winner, the thing that really matters is shaping into an outer winner. How to apply the key elements of empathy and social skills, with a focus on communication, influence, persuasion and handling objection, is the theme of this chapter. This chapter is the second step in transforming your life.

Chapter 4: Problem Solving

This chapter deals with the seven-step problem solving method. This is the third step in transforming your life.

Chapter 5: Re-engineering Yourself

To re-engineer oneself, one needs to strengthen the dimensions of an inner and outer winner. One key skill that is addressed in this chapter is the application of the situational leadership model while leading others to solve problems and produce results and create group synergy. This chapter is the fourth step in transforming your life.

Chapter 6: Growing to Serve

This chapter deals with the power of executive coaching and how that can be used to make a difference to the people you work with. This chapter contains questions and answers related to leadership development and transformation. This chapter is the fifth step in transforming your life.

Chapter 7: Serving to Grow

This chapter explains the SERVE model of leadership and the key points that a leader has to keep in mind to make his teams deliver high performance. This is the sixth step in transforming your life.

Chapter 8: Wrap Up

The last chapter captures the learning of all the previous chapters through a diagram. It also stresses the importance of values through some more FAQs.

How to use this book

Whether to read from beginning to end or in any order, I would say read it how you find comfortable. To derive maximum benefit from this book, implement the action points written at the end of each chapter in your daily life. To get an understanding on the WHY of the action points, dwell upon the diagrams/models in the chapter and their logical connections. As an author, I acknowledge the contributions of self-help pioneers like Stephen

Covey, Ken Blanchard, Spencer Johnson and Daniel Goleman that have shaped my thinking in writing this book.

At the end of the book, there are tables that list books to read, movies to watch and some training programs to attend. Do make it a point to study them as a part of your learning plan over a period of time as it would benefit you in your personal development journey.

I thought of writing this book in 2008 when I was heading the Learning & Development department at Dr. Reddy's Laboratories and driving their leadership development efforts. But for some reason it did not happen. I did not find the time. Maybe I was not inspired enough to write. But the idea of the book kept evolving. My experiences varied over the last 16 years and involved training leaders at every level in various organizations, training the medical community and also B-school students. These experiences kept adding to the design and outline of the book. It is said that every idea has its time and place. When I was instrumental in building Narsee Monjee Institute of Management Studies (NMIMS), Hyderabad, for five years as its Founder Director, I decided to pen this book.

Now, a full-time professor of Leadership, Change Management and Strategy at NMIMS, Hyderabad, I am into teaching, research and also consulting. I have designed and delivered several management development programs for banks, companies and institutions in the area of leadership over the years. As a part of my continued intellectual contribution, today I feel happy that the book has finally taken shape and found its way into your hands, reader. I believe that this book will transform your world.

Here's hoping that you will enjoy reading the book, that it will inspire you to make a positive difference in your life, that you will derive exceptional self-confidence, motivation and desire to take your organization to greater heights. And finally, that it will inspire you to make a positive difference in the communities that you live in.

All the very best towards winning in your life and career!

CHAPTER | 1

CHALLENGES

A ship is safe in harbor, but that's not what ships are for.

— John A. Shedd

There was a young man, Dev, who wanted to win in life. He had just finished college, was in his early twenties and had taken up a job. He aspired to make it big. He wanted to rise up the corporate ladder and become a CEO one day. He had dreams and the innate confidence to do it. He never doubted himself.

As he progressed in his career, he enjoyed the highs from getting promoted. But there were also times when he felt that he should have gotten a promotion and did not. During these occasions, he would feel stuck and would not know what to do next. One of his well-wishers, a friend of his father, advised him to meet a retired, wise, old man, who had had a successful career. Dev decided to meet him at the earliest.

Dev was clear about his ambitions, that he wanted to develop as a leader. So he prepared a few questions related to leadership development for the old man. He called up the veteran and fixed a meeting.

On the appointed day, Dev went to the old man's house, which was in a nice little quiet neighbourhood of the town. The old man received him pleasantly and seated him comfortably in the living room before switching off the soft music that was playing in the background. He then asked Dev what prompted him to visit.

Dev talked about his educational background. That he had studied in the best institutions in India — IIT and IIM. That he had started his career with a dream to make it big in the corporate world. While he had tasted success in the initial two years of his career where he moved from being a management trainee to an assistant manager, he now felt stuck. But he was aware that he had to move upwards and develop himself as a leader. So he wanted the wise old man to teach him about leadership development.

How to Develop As a Leader?

The wise old man listened to Dev intently and patiently. He then told Dev that he used to feel the same way when he was his age. During those times, he used to ask himself, "What is the next challenge that I could take up?" He used to take the initiative and ask his superiors to provide him with such challenges and opportunities.

Dev asked, "So leadership development takes place by seeking challenges?" The old man replied, "That is not enough. While a situation provides challenges, not everyone is willing to take up challenges with the same intensity."

Then Dev said, "So, what you are saying is that if I take up challenges and I am willing, then leadership development happens." The wise old man replied that he was not completely right. He said that challenge and willingness are necessary conditions, but not sufficient.

Dev asked, "What is the sufficient condition?" The old man said, "For full leadership development, the sufficient condition is the support that the individual receives from the organization in terms of training and mentoring. Training may also include having to read books, watch movies and make notes for oneself." He then took a piece of paper on which he drew a picture of three circles with the word WIN at the centre as shown below.

Dev found the answer to the question that he had been seeking: How does leadership development take place? Or how does an ordinary employee develop into a leader? He understood that all the three pieces needed to come together — challenge, willingness and support — for leadership development to take place.

> He understood that all the three pieces need to come together — challenge, willingness and support — for leadership development to take place.

He abbreviated the three as CWS Framework (Challenge, Willingness and Support), thanked the old man and left with a strong resolve that he would shape his career and life on this paradigm and soar like an eagle.

Much later, after thirty years, when Dev reflected on his life's journey, he perceived that the CWS Framework explained his ups and downs. Sometimes he forgot the principle and that's when he went down. At times he succeeded without his realizing because he unconsciously applied the principle. But when he did it consciously, his outcomes were as he had desired. Dev also understood that everyone constantly moves from stages of unconscious incompetence to conscious incompetence. A mentor comes and tells you that you are incompetent in a particular skill and that you need to master it. And when this fact hits you, you build the competencies and move from unconscious incompetence to conscious competence. Later, the repeated application moves you from conscious competence to unconscious competence. These are the four stages (unconscious incompetence, conscious incompetence, conscious competence, and unconscious competence) that you move through to master any skill — be it driving a car or mastering the skill of conflict resolution or for that matter anything. It pays to remember that for success, an important rule is: DESERVE before you DESIRE.

Reflecting on his life's events, Dev thought of depicting it pictorially. He took a paper and drew a graph. Not happy with the first version, he drew and redrew to come up with the final version as shown in the diagram below.

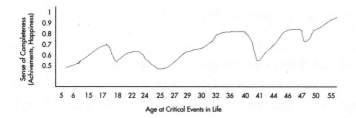

X-axis: Refers to the age at critical events took place in one's life

Y-axis: A sense of completeness (achievement, happiness) – while it is easy to measure academically, how about in professional life? Is it only promotion that translates to a sense of achievement or is there something more? The spirit of completeness is in terms of achievement and happiness and that self-assessment is represented here.

Having drawn the life's journey pictorially, he could see for himself that when the curve went up, it did so because he had done something positive, like reading a powerful book that inspired him. Similarly, sometimes his father's words profoundly influenced him. At other times, a memorable quote from Swami Vivekananda – "Take responsibility on your shoulders and you are the creator of your destiny" – inspired him. Still at other times, he watched TV programs like *Dance India Dance* or a movie like *Cast Away* that inspired him. And yet at other times, an unknown stranger would have said something that impacted him. All these instances were nothing but supporters in disguise of the CWS Framework, and it resulted in the curve going up. It is just that one needed the eyes and ears to perceive such wisdom. Having perceived and taken it seriously, Dev then walked with that wisdom to create the desired impact. *The tables of suggested books, movies and training in the annexure may serve as useful tools in your leadership journey (like that of Dev).*

Dev could now see clearly why the curve went down. He noted that deep down, he overlooked willingness and the deep desire to create an impact. He noted that in this fast-paced life, he ignored or underestimated the challenge. At other times, he took on challenges without adequate preparation. He took on responsibilities beyond his competencies. He also perceived that he was not adequately helped by his superior, with the right mentoring, the right staff or knowledge on the process, which led to a fall in the curve. But then he only had himself to blame. He should have sought advice and support from his superior, asked for adequate staff and sought clarifications on the process. That is what a winner does. In simple words, a winner has a plan. He has no excuses. A winner knows that the problem is in the mirror and the solution is in the mirror, too. That is, himself.

To rise from the ashes, Dev noted that he has to transform himself. Taking the responsibility of changing oneself is not an easy path. It is a difficult journey. It is just like a caterpillar having to go through the painful process of shedding its skin to become a butterfly. No pain, no gain. It is like the story of the eagle. A typical eagle lives for forty-five years. By this age, its feathers become weak. So it becomes difficult for it to fly and catch its prey. Its beak and talons become blunt. So it becomes difficult to peck at the prey that it catches. Then the eagle has a choice. Either to wither and die or live for another thirty years by going through a painful process of shedding its feathers and peeling away its talons and beak by scratching against rocks. The process is painful. But it is only by going through this process that the eagle gets new feathers, new beak and new talons after five months. And now, it is ready once again to soar high, fly with speed, catch its prey and eat. Are you willing to go through this pain and training in your life constantly so that you win the game of life? Are you ready to be the CHANGE that you wish to see for yourself!

Are you willing to go through this pain and training in your life constantly so that you win the game of life? Are you ready to be the CHANGE that you wish to see for yourself!

Discover, Learn and Apply to Win

Dev had completed his Master's degree in Business Administration. He had mastered the knowledge (what to, why to) in the fields of strategy, marketing, finance, operations and human resources. As he started applying the knowledge, he developed the skills (how to). Over time, repeated application of the knowledge and skills that sprouted from his attitude (willingness to) helped him master the craft of management and get superior results.

Dev had the habit of writing notes to himself. He maintained a journal. He realized that when he wrote, his thinking crystallized. At one such time, he penned down the concept of attitude, skill and knowledge. He had the habit of reflecting and remembering by writing down acronyms. In that instant, the acronym was ASK: A for Attitude, S for Skill and K for Knowledge. He recognized that Knowledge has to precede Skill, but for easy remembrance, he stacked away the concept in his memory as ASK.

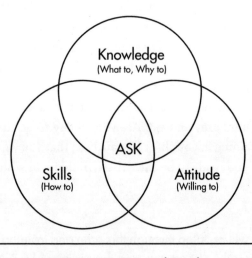

He then deliberated further and asked himself whether he can come up with a new model that combined the ASK diagram with the previous CWS diagram. The outcome is the one drawn below that started making immense sense for Dev. The model below explained the framework towards winning. Dev felt happy that he could go back to this model in times of crisis as a diagnostic tool to correct the situation. When not winning, one or a few of the six pieces (challenge, willingness, support, attitude, knowledge and skills) may be missing and he had to work on those pieces to get the desired results.

In his mid-thirties, ten years into his career, Dev read a powerful book, *The Fifth Discipline* by Peter Senge. The concept of five disciplines in the book shaped his thinking further. He came up with the below diagram, an adapted version from Peter Senge's work. The diagram started providing greater insights to his life's challenges.

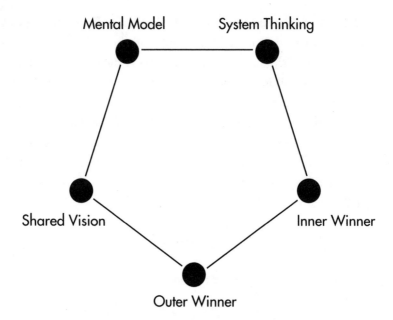

Mental Model System Thinking

Shared Vision Inner Winner

Outer Winner

Five Disciplines

Having done his MBA, Dev acquired knowledge in strategy, marketing, finance, operations and human resources through case study discussions, assignments and projects. In his today's job, those concepts and frameworks made a lot of sense.

For each management function, Dev narrowed down to three to five key mental models. For instance, in the subject of Strategy, Dev internalized the mental models of SWOT (Strengths, Weaknesses, Opportunities and Threats), 5 Forces (Porter's Diagram for industry analysis), Differentiation and PEST (Political, Economic, Social and Technological). Similarly in the subject of Marketing, Dev felt that mental models of STP (Segmentation, Targeting and Positioning), 4 Ps (Product, Price, Place and Promotion), etc., resonated well with him. More than the quantum of knowledge, it is those few cutting edge mental models that served as powerful tools in making sense of the complex world and taking decisions. These mental models were like algorithms that helped him take decisions and act with a high probability of success. His two years study of these subjects along with the business simulations taught him to develop a systems thinking, appreciate and understand the cause-effect relationships.

> For each function of management, Dev narrowed down to three to five key mental models.

The hard skills acquired through application of knowledge in areas like finance, marketing and operations had to be supplemented with soft skills developed through the application of knowledge in human resources.

It is akin to what happens in the medical field. A budding doctor is expected to have subject knowledge, competency in acquiring skills (procedures performed, assisted/observed), emergency duties, clinical bedside discussions, outpatient department work, in patient department work, punctuality and attendance, public relations and teamwork, and participation in seminars/conferences/CME/organizational procedures.

It is the hard and soft skills that make a difference to win in life. Hard skills without soft skills have a limited impact and vice-versa. It is a continuous journey and these skills need to be honed by playing the game of life at bigger and more challenging levels.

Your persona is a result of AKS (Attitude, Knowledge, Skill).

Knowledge and experience result in developing mental models and systems thinking in a particular area. Application of the knowledge becomes a skill or competency and behaviour.

Where knowledge and skill are built on strong bedrock of right attitude, the achievement of goals is outstanding. Knowledge and skills are easier to acquire and change, but the same is not the case for adopting the right attitude.

Getting Started

The right attitude develops by becoming an inner winner and outer winner, the theme of the second and the third chapter. The fourth chapter focuses on the generic method of problem solving in the context of the challenges in your knowledge area. It is the formula for converting the knowledge in your technical area into a skill.

The subsequent chapters will complete your understanding

AREA FOR MASTERY	HUMAN RESOURCE MANAGEMENT(I)	TECHNICAL	HUMAN RESOURCE MANAGEMENT(II)	CONCEPTUAL
PRIMARY THEME	*Understanding & Leading Self* *Ingredients for the right ATTITUDE*	*BASIC Ingredient for mental models and systems thinking in the technical area* *Technical/ Management – Sales, Marketing, Operations, Finance, HR*	*Influencing others* *Ingredient for mental models and systems thinking in influencing people*	*Leading a Group/ Organization* *Ingredient for mental models and systems thinking in influencing people, having a shared vision and collectively moving towards common goals*
SKILLS	Applying the knowledge of Inner Winner and Outer Winner	Applying the knowledge of Problem Solving	Applying the knowledge of Re-engineering and GROW	Applying the knowledge of SERVE Model
KNOWLEDGE	Inner winner Outer winner	Problem Solving	Re-engineering GROW	SERVE Model

on what makes one win. The fifth chapter on re-engineering primarily deals with the situational leadership while the sixth chapter on GROW deals with coaching and mentoring.

The seventh chapter on SERVE to Grow conceptualizes the mind-set and thought processes related to leading, contributing and serving. It is placed in the below picture as a PLATFORM, as the basic purpose of our existence is to manage, live, lead and serve.

The entire framework of this book is built on eight chapters. The linkage between the key concepts (challenge, willingness and support) in this first chapter and the subsequent chapters is shown below.

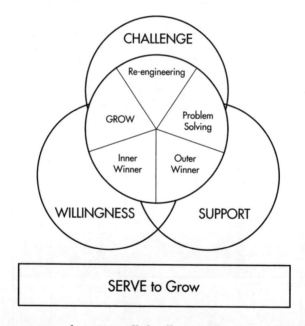

The next two chapters will dwell upon the art and science of becoming an inner winner and outer winner that form two of the five disciplines just now discussed.

Dev also started seeing his role more comprehensively in terms of WORK and LIFE. He started seeing his life in a 360-degree way as below.

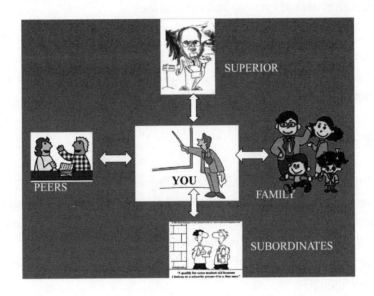

This picture made him feel more complete with his roles and goals. It started dawning on him to run his own race, a race that resonated with his inner strengths and competencies.

You would note that you need to take good care of the job that you are assigned, of the relationship with your superior, subordinates and peers. Not to forget taking good care of your family, friends and relatives.

There is something missing in the above picture. Can you guess what it is?

Yes, what is missing is indeed the self. Unless you take good care of yourself, you will not be happy. Unless you are happy, you cannot make others happy. This is fundamental.

So the question comes: "When are you happy?" You are happy when you achieve, whatever that project maybe at work. And you achieve when you are mentally alert, which springs from a healthy habit of exercise and meditation.

Therefore the adage 'Do take good care of yourself,' is of paramount importance. "*I take good care of myself and therefore I am strong. Now I can take good care of others. This insight is so fundamental that we tend to overlook in the 'busy'ness of life.*"

Key Points

The three pieces of challenge, willingness and support (CWS) are like the three legs of a stool. All the three are necessary and sufficient conditions. Even if one of them is not there, the stool will not stand. In other words, do not expect successful outcomes or good results without the operation of challenge, willingness and support.

At the centre of the CWS Framework is knowledge, skill and attitude, i.e., ASK or KSA.

Knowledge and skills result in developing mental models and systems thinking in a particular area; the two disciplines out of the five that you need to master to win in career and life. The other three disciplines are the inner winner, the outer winner and shared vision.

The entire framework of this book is built on eight chapters. The linkage between the key concepts (challenge, willingness and support) in this first chapter and the subsequent chapters is shown on page 14.

* You will note that there are six chapters, following the first chapter that explain the six steps to transform your life. The chapters relate to Inner Winner, Outer Winner, Problem Solving, Re-engineering Yourself, Grow to Serve and Serve to Grow. The last chapter is the conclusion.

Action Points for You

1. Draw up your life's journey like in the second diagram of the chapter. It is immaterial how old you are now. Take in account your school days till now.

2. Do you see the ups and downs? You do not need to be an expert to figure out the answers behind the ups and downs. Be candid and truthful with yourself.

3. Now at this point in your life, draw the 360-degree profile as noted in the last diagram of this chapter.

4. For each of the relationships in the 360-degree profile, come up with plans to nurture them!

5. Last but not the least, do not forget to take good care of yourself.

CHAPTER | **2**

Inner Winner

When the need to succeed is as bad as the need to breathe, then you will be successful

— Eric Thomas

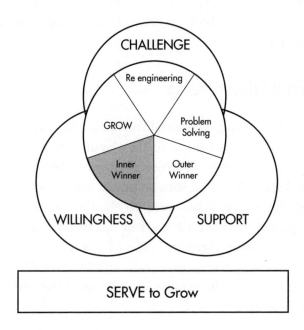

Post-independence, India adopted a mixed economy model based on a combination of socialism and capitalism. Prime Minister Jawaharlal Nehru of the Congress Party in 1950s built the modern temples of India — hydroelectric dams and steel plants — to usher in agricultural revolution and speed up industrial growth. The commanding heights of the economy in terms of defence and infrastructure were given a boost through the setup of public sector units. Contrary to critics' prediction that India will not be able to govern itself, the country progressed based on the founding principles of democracy, secularism, self-reliance and poverty alleviation.

It was during this time Dev was born in Hyderabad, in the early sixties. His dad was a doctor working at the government hospital during the day and doing private practice at night. Dev was fortunate to be born to devoted parents with two loving brothers and a sister.

The First Fifteen Years

In 1960-70s, during Dev's childhood, the country witnessed war with China over a disputed Himalayan territory. India lost that war, but annexed the former Portuguese Indian territories of Goa, Daman and Diu, with an armed action carried out by the Indian army in December 1961. In 1964, Prime Minister Nehru passed away. In 1965, when Lal Bahadur Shastri was the prime minister, there was a second war with Pakistan over Kashmir, the first having been fought in 1948. In 1968, Nehru's daughter Indira Gandhi became Prime Minister after the sudden demise of Shastri.

As a child, Dev had always got what he wanted. His father would buy him toys and Dev would enjoy playing with them. He would read the *Amar Chitra Katha* comics and got inspired from the *Ramayana* and the *Mahabharata*. The character of Lord Krishna fascinated him so much that he insisted on dressing up as the Lord, complete with the flute, and even had photographs taken. On another occasion, at Dev's persuasion, his uncles and mother constructed a miniature glass temple in which the family deity, Tirupati Balaji, was kept. Once, on a tour to the local Nizam's exhibition, again on Dev's request, his parents purchased a beautiful yellow Buddha, which later adorned the house.

Looking back, Dev was thankful to his parents for his nurtured upbringing. Despite his busy schedule at the hospital as well as his active private practice at home, Dev's father used to take the children to the library and recreation centre. Dev learned to swim there. Some afternoons were spent in simply singing songs. Dev's father encouraged his children to participate in extra-curricular activities. They also adopted two wonderful dogs. It was natural for Dev's mother to give shelter to almost every abandoned cat in the neighbourhood. Through these animals, the children learned to care and share.

One of the best things that Dev's father did was to take his children to Ramakrishna Math. The values that defined Dev later were shaped by the influence of Swami Ranganathananda, the writings of Swami Vivekananda and the conversations with his own father. When they went on long drives to their village, Dev would receive nuggets of wisdom from his father. At a young age, Dev learned that work was to be worshipped. Dev's father was an ideal role model for his children with his dint of discipline, hard work, balanced life and love for books.

Dev was made self-reliant and independent from an early age. By the time he was twelve, he had started cycling to school that was five kilometres away. Not once did he remember his father telling him to study for exams. Instead, he reminisced about his father always telling his mother to let the children sleep well so that they could perform well in their exams. Dev did not attend the first grade because he had an exceptional IQ and was admitted directly into the second grade from Upper Kindergarten (UKG). However, it took him another three years to catch up and top the class. Dev distinctly remembered the encouragement he received from his father during his childhood. Once, Dev had to tell his father about his mediocre academic performance. His father responded by saying, "Well done! You are among the top ten. Going forward, you can aim to be among the top three." And his father's words motivated him. By the time Dev went to the fifth grade, he started topping the class consistently and culminated by getting state honors in the tenth grade board examination. Those positive strokes from his father and the high standards set by his brothers made a big difference in Dev's life.

While at school, one of the best experiences that Dev had was going on an excursion to western India and visiting places like Goa and Mumbai. The camaraderie he shared with his fellow mates and the administrators of the school during the trip had a telling impact on his young mind. On returning from the excursion, Dev was indeed thankful to his father for allowing him to go.

The Next Twelve Years

Dev passed his tenth standard with flying colours, like all his brothers. Dev's father had assumed that he would pursue medicine after finishing school. But for some reason, his heart was not into biology or even zoology. Mathematics interested him. He cried the day when he was told that he should go into the biology stream. His father did not push the matter further, but left him alone and told him to think it over. When Dev did not relent and stuck to his guns, his father graciously agreed to him pursuing Mathematics. That was a defining moment for him. He felt exhilarated and went on to do exceedingly well in his academics.

The '70s was a turbulent and testing time for India. The country saw its third war with Pakistan in 1971, over the creation of Bangladesh, formerly East Pakistan. Simultaneously, India signed a twenty-year friendship treaty with the Soviet Union. In 1973, India tested its first nuclear weapon in Pokhran. In 1975, Prime Minister Indira Gandhi declared a state of emergency after being found guilty of electoral malpractice. In 1977, nearly 1,000 political opponents were imprisoned and a program of compulsory birth control was introduced. In 1978, Indira Gandhi's Congress Party lost the general election. Janata Party came to power with Morarji Desai as the prime minister. At the same time, the Communist Party of India (Marxist) came into power for the first time in West Bengal.

In that same year, Dev joined the IIT.

During his engineering days, Dev noticed a shift in his relationship with his father. He felt more comfortable, more like friends rather than father and son. Dev also started understanding that behind the strong, disciplined, exterior of his father, there was a deep loving heart.

After IIT, Dev got admission into IIM. The two-year stay at IIM helped Dev to develop his personality. During this period, he overcame stage fright by taking the initiative to present case studies. While leaving the portals of the campus, Dev told himself — *We are leaving into the unknown world outside. From this day on, I will excel at management. I will never get tired of listening to people. I will be harsh on myself, inculcate the necessary discipline and will try to become a star.*

Post his MBA, Dev decided to do IAS. He cleared the preliminaries but failed the finals. It was the first time that Dev had faced a failure. That terrible day, as Dev sat at the breakfast table and noted that his roll number had not flashed in the newspaper, he looked up to see the hurt in his father's eyes. However, he did not say anything to Dev, who felt the deep acceptance from his side and an understanding that he, Dev, who had done his best and there was nothing to worry about. Time and again, his father taught Dev that in life learn to do your best and leave the rest.

Quoting from the *Bhagavad Gita*, he used to tell Dev, "To work alone thou hast a right and not to its fruits thereof!"

Dev picked himself up from there and worked to bounce back in his chosen career of business administration. He went to Mumbai to work in the financial sector. He told himself:

If you believe in something with firm conviction, go ahead and implement it. People may trigger doubts around it. Do not let such doubts worry you. In good time, events will arrange themselves harmoniously around you.

While at his job, Dev reminded himself: *Go into the minutest details of the job. Analyze mentally; give concrete shape to these ideas verbally. What is needed is meticulous planning, whether meeting a person or a group or an organization. Thoughts always flash across. Give shape to these thoughts. Put it down in writing. There is so much to learn every day. Memorize what you learn every day. Let this be a relentless activity.*

Daily reflections led Dev to decide on a course of action for every day. He decided to: *treat every day as an opening to learn something more. At the end of the day, isolate yourself in a room and recap the day's events. At the start of day, decide the new things you are going to implement. In other words, Plan, Be and Learn for the day. Prioritize your activities through planning. Strike a balance between work and family.*

Weekly Planning

Dev started using a diary to plan and record events. He also kept a pocket book to jot down ideas. He did it consistently for ten years with some fairly good results and yet he felt something was missing with his diary-writing ritual. Around this time, he stumbled across the book *The 7 Habits of Highly Effective People* by Stephen Covey and read about 'first things first' (the third habit in the book) that gave a snapshot of a weekly planning tool that helped him fill the gap.

In the weekly planning tool (or the weekly worksheet on page 26), on the left side, there is a column that prompts the user to think about his role and goal. Then it urges to write down the weekly priorities. From here on, priorities for the week are distributed over the seven days. One can then focus on implementing the priorities to reach the desired goal.

> In the weekly planning tool, on the left side, there is a column that prompts the user to think about his role and goal.

To arrive at the priorities, Dev started using the Priorities Matrix shown below that prompted him to decide on the important and the urgent. He made it a daily habit to ask, "What are the things to be achieved for the day?"

Priorities

First Things First
(Action Plan)

"Things that matter the most must never be at the mercy of things that matter the least."

WEEKLY WORKSHEET		Week of	Sunday	Monday	Tuesday	Wednesday	Thursday	Friday	Saturday
Roles	Goals	Weekly Priorities				Today's Priorities			
						Appointments/Commitments			
			8	8	8	8	8	8	8
			9	9	9	9	9	9	9
			10	10	10	10	10	10	10
			11	11	11	11	11	11	11
			12	12	12	12	12	12	12
			1	1	1	1	1	1	1
			2	2	2	2	2	2	2
			3	3	3	3	3	3	3
			4	4	4	4	4	4	4
			5	5	5	5	5	5	5

TAKING CARE OF ME

Physical _____
Mental _____
Spiritual _____
Social/Emotional _____

	Evening	Evening	Evening	Evening	Evening	Evening	Evening
6							
7							
8							

To arrive at the priorities, Dev started using the Priorities Matrix that prompted him to decide on the important and the urgent.

	URGENT	NOT URGENT
Not Important	I ACTIVITIES Crises, Pressing problems, Deadline-driven projects	II ACTIVITIES Prevention, PC activities, Relationship building, Recognizing new opportunities, Planning recreation
Important	III ACTIVITIES Interruptions, Some calls, Some mails, Some reports, Some meetings, Pressing matters, Popular activities	IV ACTIVITIES Trivia, Busy work, Some mails, Some phone calls, Time wasters, Pleasant activities

PRIORITIES MATRIX

First, he segregated the list into important and unimportant. Having arrived at the list of important things, he then asked which are urgent and not so urgent. This kind of planning made him calm, composed and he felt in control of the situation for the day. His levels of anxiety came down. He realized that he should arrive and focus on important and not urgent. But if he had to do that, he had to arrive at important things and move them from urgent to not urgent category through planning, relationship building, prevention mind set, recognizing new opportunities, etc. The more he did that, the more he moved away from crisis situations regarding his projects. The trick is getting out of the crisis syndrome — tendency to wait till the last moment to get things done. For instance, if you are a student, prioritize advance preparation for the exam so that you are not cramming in lessons at the last minute, a thing so common among the students.

However, you will only have time to prepare a 'to-do' list if you first make a 'stop-doing' list. Ultimately, you have only 24 hours in a day. Given today's heightened competition and the need to stand out that comes from investing significant time in a particular activity and gaining mastery, the trick is narrowing down to three major goals that you want to achieve.

After a while, Dev felt that it is extremely important to have a vision even before doing the weekly plan. The long-term has to dovetail into the short-term. The long-term organizing meant writing down a mission statement and deriving the roles and goals from the mission statement. Once the long-term goals are clear, it can be converted to yearly goals and reduced to quarterly goals followed by monthly goals and weekly goals.

Once the roles and goals for the long-term are clear, it can be converted to yearly goals and reduced to quarterly goals followed by monthly goals and weekly goals.

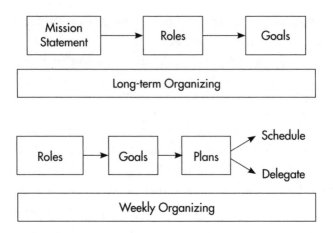

LONG-TERM TO WEEKLY

And then the weekly planning sheet gets effectively filled up. A sample weekly plan of Dev is depicted so that the reader can draw inspiration from it to prepare one himself. Notice that Dev has kept one of the roles as Individual Personal Development. His other roles combined professional and personal life. He also allocated time for community service in terms of voluntary work at the Ramakrishna Math. Last but not the least, Dev spent one hour daily doing exercises — walking, yoga, breathing and meditation. Investing this one hour helped Dev to feel energized throughout the day, which made a huge positive impact on his work and other activities.

First Things First

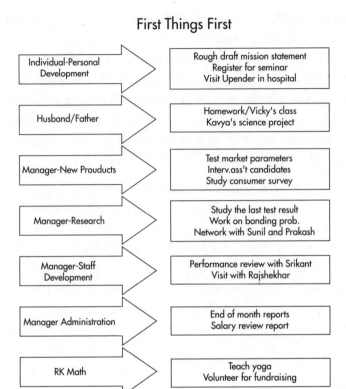

Individual-Personal Development	Rough draft mission statement Register for seminar Visit Upender in hospital
Husband/Father	Homework/Vicky's class Kavya's science project
Manager-New Prouducts	Test market parameters Interv.ass't candidates Study consumer survey
Manager-Research	Study the last test result Work on bonding prob. Network with Sunil and Prakash
Manager-Staff Development	Performance review with Srikant Visit with Rajshekhar
Manager Administration	End of month reports Salary review report
RK Math	Teach yoga Volunteer for fundraising

The key to effectiveness is arriving at the purpose and writing down the mission statement. The big question is, how do you arrive at it?

The key is arriving at the purpose and writing down the mission statement.

It begins with understanding yourself, knowing your unique strengths and competencies. Your current strengths would have accumulated from the choices that you had made earlier. For instance, an MBA student might have made a choice to specialize in Finance and marketing in order to reach a position of eminence in the financial services industry. It comes from asking (i) What am I best at? (ii) What do I love doing? (iii) Can I convert my competence and passion for an activity into money? Constant reflection and guidance from a mentor can go a long way in answering these critical questions. It is all about discovering the diamond in you and then "acing" in your life.

This same framework of questions would be applicable at various stages to the student who has just graduated from college and is on his professional journey. Dev realized the strategic importance of these seemingly simple questions and regularly kept asking them once every three years. And it made a big difference! It gave him a sense of direction. It helped him take stock of the as-is position (initial position) and gave a line of sight for the future in terms of to-be position (future position). It gave clarity on what needs to be done and what skills need to be picked up to go from initial to future position in a specified time frame.

What are Guiding Values?

While Dev went about his daily chores, at times doing things differently and rewriting rules, he realized that it is important to take decisions based on guiding values. He asked himself, "What are values? What do I value as an individual?" He remembered the wise old man, and to get the answers to this question, he went to meet him once again.

In the conversation that ensued, the old man asked Dev whether he knew the story of the *Mahabharata* and why different characters took sides with either the Kauravas or the Pandavas.

When asked why Bhishma, the grand old warrior, fought with the Kauravas, Dev could not come up with an answer. The man then revealed that Bhishma took an oath that he would not marry, would not sit on the throne but instead, protect the person sitting on the throne of Hastinapura. It is for this reason that Bhishma fought with Kauravas, who were the rulers of Hastinapura. Bhishma valued his oath. He knew that righteousness or dharma was on the Pandavas' side and yet he fought with the Kauravas because he valued standing by his oath and considered it more important than dharma.

Next, the man asked Dev why Karna fought on the side of the Kauravas knowing fully well that righteousness was on the side of the Pandavas. Dev answered that Karna valued Duryodhana's friendship far more than dharma. To the question why Drona fought on the side of the Kauravas, the answer was loyalty.

Finally came the question why Lord Kirshna fought on the side of the Pandavas. The answer was simple – Krishna valued righteousness or dharma more than anything else. That is the reason why he fought on the side of the Pandavas.

Dev could then clearly understand the meaning of values. He learnt that values are those that are dear to your heart; something that cannot be given up under any circumstances; are uncompromising and unwavering. He once again thanked the wise old man for his time and left with greater zeal towards work and life.

He learnt that values are those that are dear to your heart; something that cannot be given up under any circumstances; are uncompromising and unwavering.

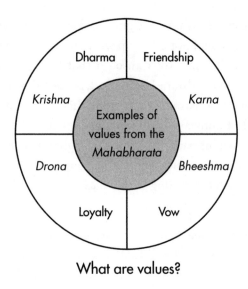

What are values?

While working, Dev told himself that he has to lead life with values. While writing his journal, he penned: "Develop the philosophy and principles of your life along the inputs provided by Indian ethos. Sit down and meditate upon 'What should be my guiding values?' Respect these values. Write these values down, hang it on the wall and practice them. Live and champion the values."

After a bit of introspection, Dev arrived at the following values for himself: career growth, discipline, integrity, relationships, wealth and personal development. There were several others that popped into his mind, but he wanted to keep it simple and reduce the set to six that really mattered.

When Dev read *The Road Less Travelled* by Scott Peck, he could not help but feel extremely motivated. Discipline is the product of delay in gratification and time invested in building competencies with the aim of achieving self-reliance.

A Winner's Mindset

In one of the training programmes that Dev attended, he was prompted to ask himself WHO AM I? Am I the professional or the son or the father or the husband? The ultimate answer distilled down to I AM THE WORD. And for Dev, the WORD was the Purpose/Mission and Values. He needed to commit to a purpose and work as if his life depended on it. When one declared the purpose in front of several people, and it is not easy doing so because it needed courage, then one became an actor on the stage and not a spectator in the balcony. From there emanates the roles, goals and the weekly planning in one's life. And as time passes by, there may be breakthroughs or breakdowns. Dev started getting a holistic view of himself and he drew an image as below. *That is ME!* Dev smiled to himself.

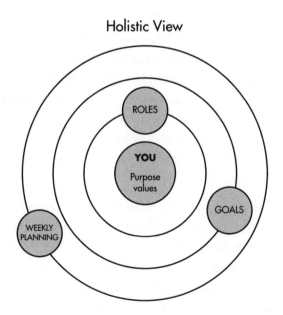

Holistic View

With a clear sense of purpose, roles and goals, plans become realistic. With values to guide one's decisions, the plans become rooted in reality. A clear sense of purpose unleashes energy and enthusiasm. It also drives one to make the optimum use of the available resources and work with creative imagination. In that state, one gets to understand the deeper meaning of resourcefulness where one can leverage the meagre resources for maximum impact through sheer willpower and concentration. YOU at the centre is your proactive nature, your energy and enthusiasm. YOU is the ability to energize others, live on the edge and execute. YOU, in short, is your winner's mindset.

> With a clear sense of purpose, roles and goals, plans
> become realistic. With values to guide one's decisions,
> the plans become rooted in reality.

A winner has a plan whereas a loser has excuses. A winner is proactive whereas a loser is reactive. A winner sees a glass as half full whereas a loser sees the glass as half empty. A winner sees a solution in every problem whereas a loser sees a problem in every solution. It is for you to decide which of the two mindsets you would like to have. You have the freedom to choose. The diagram below is courtesy of Stephen Covey's book *The 7 Habits of Highly Effective People*.

The freedom to choose is in between the space between stimulus and response. It is based on a bedrock of self-awareness, creative imagination, will and consciousness. When you lose (stimulus), you have the freedom to choose — to get up to fight or give up (response). Great leaders like Abraham Lincoln and Mahatma Gandhi exercised the freedom to choose constantly

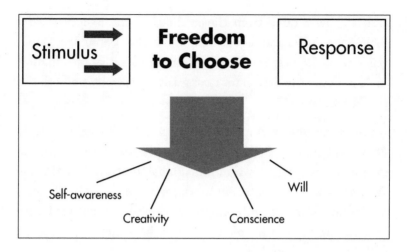

with a winner's mindset. Lincoln faced several setbacks before he got elected as the president of the United States. It was also at a critical time when the northern and southern states were fighting over the issue of slavery. At every setback, Lincoln chose to get up and fight, not lose heart but persist. Lincoln operated with a winner's mindset and remained proactive throughout his time as President.

Gandhi, when he returned to India from South Africa, used Satyagraha (non-violence) as a means the end the British raj. He tested Satyagraha in 1906 in South Africa and had successful results. He therefore tried it in India. Gandhi took the freedom movement from the classes to the masses. He identified with them more and took the difficult decision of donning meagre clothes. He led by example. He was authentic. People trusted him. His aura was so powerful that people simply obeyed his call, whether he was pro- or anti-boycotting. Gandhi, like Lincoln, knew he had complete freedom for decision-making. All his decisions and actions sprouted from this freedom to choose. His self-awareness and willpower came from the readings of the *Bhagavad Gita*, Bible, meditation and regular long walks. The Dandi Salt March was one of the best instances of Gandhi's creative imagination as he opposed the British for taxing salt, a necessity for both the rich and the poor.

The same winner's mindset is a popular theme for many Bollywood movies. The film *Iqbal* narrates the story of a young man in a small rural town in India. Iqbal, portrayed by Shreyas Talpade, is deaf and mute. But he aspires to be a great bowler. His mother and sister secretly support his ambitions, but his father does not agree with his plans. Instead, he wants Iqbal to work with him in the family farm. One day, Iqbal gets thrown out of the local team as a result of petty politics. With no trainer, he has to fend for himself. At this point, he comes across a retired bowler, played by Naseeruddin Shah, who lost interest in life and is an alcoholic. Iqbal requests him to coach him. The story unfolds to show the triumph of the human spirit against all odds. Iqbal displays a winner's mindset at every obstacle that he faces on his road to play the game at the national level.

Another film, *Chhoti Si Baath*, motivated Dev. The story revolves around a diffident young working man falling in love with a working woman. He is shy and fails to express himself to her. And there is a competitor who is always one up on him. The young man finds a mentor who helps him win the girl's hand. The movie is all about overcoming one's weaknesses, facing life with confidence and achieving the goals that one has set for oneself.

Dev asked himself, can I exercise the freedom to choose and develop a winner's mindset? Can I bulletproof myself with a winner's mindset? Can I develop the power of positive thinking? His father and his father's close friend have been a source of inspiration to Dev all along. Whenever the going got tough,

Dev remembered the travails that these two gentlemen went through in shaping their lives and then his difficulties seemed less burdensome. Dev's father always advised him to lead life with equanimity. Peaks and valleys are a natural part of one's life. Do not get too depressed when in the valley nor too elated when on the peak. Learn to lead life with poise and balance. While the outer state may be turbulent, learn and practice to keep the inner state calm. This makes one bulletproof against the vicissitudes of life.

Dev took time to know himself better. He asked the human resources department in his office to guide him on this aspect. There were several instruments available, like the Myers Briggs Type Indicator (MBTI), Fundamental Interrelationships Behaviour (FIRO-B), DISC, etc. Dev took all these tests. He also made it a point to seek feedback from the people around him. Slowly and surely, he could see his areas of strength and also his blind spots (areas where he felt he was good but the people around perceived him to be not so, and desired to improve). With affirmations, Dev started overcoming his blind spots. While reversing the blind spots may be extremely difficult, just to be aware of it makes a difference. Dev also saw that it was much easier to strengthen the strengths rather than convert weaknesses into strengths.

> He also made it a point to seek feedback from the people around him. With affirmations, Dev started overcoming his blind spots.

At a much later time, after 20 years, Dev saw the film *3 Idiots*. In the movie, the hero Ranchoddas Chanchad famously tells that when tense before exams or some other critical time, remind your good self by tapping on the heart "All is well". Quite a few training programs emphasize on the importance of positive affirmation. One such useful affirmation is, "Day by day, in every way, I am more and more healthy, wealthy, loving, peaceful and enlightened."

During one telephone call with his Dad, Dev was advised by him to go to the Ramakrishna Math to pick up a few books on the works of Swami Vivekananda on Vedanta and Upanishads. These works emphasize the importance of strength, fearlessness and faith in oneself. In fact, these qualities are the very hallmarks of a winner.

A few powerful quotes of Swamiji can serve as useful affirmations in one's daily existence as a winner:

"Purity, perseverance and patience are the three essentials to success."

"Faith, faith, faith in oneself and faith, faith in God is the secret to greatness."

"Education is the manifestation of perfection already in man."

"To be good and do good is the essence of whole religion."

"Mediate in silence and become a dynamo of spirituality."

"Take the whole responsibility on your shoulders and know that you are the creator of your own destiny."

Make it a point to read autobiographies of a few people whom you admire. Dev read Dr. A.P.J. Abdul Kalam's autobiography *Wings of Fire* and was greatly influenced by it. He read about Dr. Venkataswamy of Aravind Eye Care who pursued the mission of eradicating needless blindness and built an institution of international eminence in Madurai, Coimbatore and other parts of South India.

During the 80s, India witnessed Indira Gandhi's return to power, heading Congress Party's splinter group, Congress (I). In 1983, N. T. Rama Rao's one-month-old Telugu Desam Party came to power in Andhra Pradesh, marking a new challenger, post Jayaprakash Narayan against Mrs. Gandhi. During that year, Mrs. Gandhi ordered Operation Blue Star. Army troops stormed the Golden Temple — the Sikh holy shrine — to flush out Sikh militants pressing for self-rule. In 1984, Indira Gandhi was assassinated by her own Sikh bodyguards, following which there were riots. Riding the sympathy wave, her son, Rajiv, took over as Prime Minister. In 1987, India deployed troops for peacekeeping operation in Sri Lanka's ethnic conflict. With the Bofors scandal in 1988 and falling public support, Congress was defeated in the general election. In 1989, National Front (India) headed by N. T. Rama Rao stormed to power with outside support from BJP and CPI. V.P. Singh became the prime minister of India.

While Dev was working in Mumbai, his parents and sister found a girl for him. Dev, along with his parents, visited the girl and her family. It was an instant yes from both of them and their wedding was fixed.

Dev went to invite the wise old man for his wedding. During their chat, the old man told Dev that he is on the path of being an inner winner. To succeed on the outside, you need to win on the inside. Just as algebra precedes calculus, becoming an inner winner precedes becoming an outer one. It is inside first and outside next. Becoming an inner winner requires purpose and values, roles and goals and exercising the freedom to choose and taking initiative.

For Dev, the wise old man was a role model and a mentor because he demonstrated continuous personal growth and helped Dev find answers to questions that troubled him, and also constantly motivated him.

The day of the nuptials arrived. The wise old man attended the ceremony and blessed the couple.

Key Points

To become an inner winner, you need to work on four things (1) Weekly planning (2) Writing your purpose/mission statement and also values that guide your decisions (3) Exercising the freedom to choose and developing a winner's mindset (4) The power of taking feedback and using autosuggestions to boost the strengths and overcome the weaknesses.

This chapter is the first step towards transforming your life.

Action Points for You

1. Begin with planning for the week. Please note that it is not planning for the day but planning for the week. It takes around 45 minutes to do by sitting in a quiet corner on a Sunday morning. It sounds easy but difficult to practice. Practice it for four weeks and you will notice the difference.

2. Reflect and meditate; write down your statement of purpose or your mission statement. It will give direction to the roles and goals.

3. Take time to ponder over what you value in life. These values will help guide your daily decision making.

4. Read the books listed in the table in the appendix so as to develop a winner's mindset. Some of the suggested books are (i) *Think and Grow Rich* (ii) *The Power of Positive Thinking*.

5. Read biographies/autobiographies of people whom you admire and see as role models.

CHAPTER | 3

Outer Winner

We are what we repeatedly do. Excellence, then, is not an act, but a habit.

— Aristotle

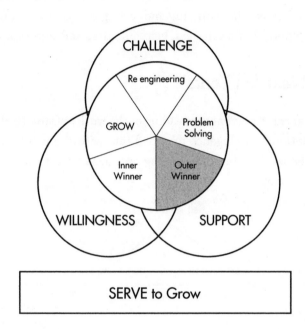

Dev changed jobs and shifted to a different city. His new role involved higher responsibilities, like leading a team. From an individual contributor, he became a team leader.

He had no training to shoulder the responsibilities of a leader. He realized that it was a completely different ball game. He reflected over the fact that it was easier to do your tasks as an individual and have no responsibility for the results of others. But once he became a team leader, he was responsible for the results of others. He had to learn the hard way to change his mindset, to be genuinely happy for a team member's success. It is natural for us to envy the achievements of others, be it our own team member or more so one's peers. Dev asked himself, "Can I develop that sense of belongingness where I see myself winning with the achievement of my team member and passing the credit and reward to that member? How do I bring that behavioural change? How do I evoke that thinking and feeling authentically? How do I bring about that awareness, belongingness and commitment?"

The Next Ten Years

It was at this time that the reading of the work of Daniel Goleman on emotional intelligence provided him with the mental model that shaped his thinking, feeling and behaviour to become an outer winner.

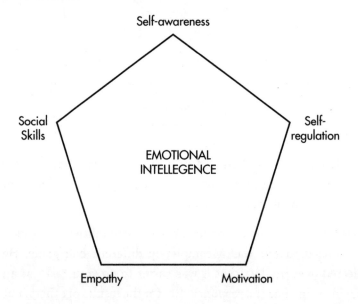

Empathy and Social Skills

The two key skills that he read, understood and applied were empathy and social skills. These key points clubbed with his earlier reading of Stephen Covey's *The 7 Habits of Highly Effective People* helped him progressively to become an outer winner.

The two key skills that he read, understood and applied were empathy and social skills.

Dev could not help but write down the key elements and then map them in the works of Stephen Covey and Daniel Goleman. He mapped the points in the following table to crystallize his thinking.

Around this time, Dev got an opportunity for mobilizing funds for his company. To fund the expansion and meet the capital expenditure, the company explored various financial options. With his prior experience in capital markets, Dev worked on the financial proposal and made a winning presentation to the top management. The proposal got accepted and a six-month deadline was set to raise the money through financial institutions and public offerings. A project charter was prepared and under the mentorship of his boss, Dev worked like a man possessed. He travelled every week to Mumbai, the mecca of financial markets. Week after week, he visited various financial institutions for underwriting, interacted closely with the lead managers to the issue and made relevant submissions to Securities Exchange Board of India, worked together with the financial intermediaries to market and sell the public offering. The D-Day arrived, the day of the opening of the issue. The offering was oversubscribed. The success of the IPO led to the recognition of Dev's excellent contribution and earned him his promotion.

On silent reflection, Dev realized that the success and rewards that followed happened due to the application of the key

	DANIEL GOLEMAN	STEPHEN COVEY
Inside – inner winner	Self-awareness	Emotional awareness, accurate self-assessment, self confidence	Habit 1 – Be proactive
	Self-regulation	Self-control, trustworthiness, conscientiousness, adaptability, innovation	Habit 1 – Be proactive
	Motivation	Achievement, commitment, initiative, optimism	Habit 2 – Begin with the end in mind
			Habit 3 – First things first
Outside – outer winner	Empathy	Understanding others, developing others, service orientation, leveraging diversity, political awareness	Habit 5 – Seek to understand than be understood
	Social skills	Influence, communication, conflict management	Habit 4 – Think win-win and Habit 6 –Synergize
		Leadership, change catalyst, building bonds, collaboration and cooperation, team capabilities	

elements of the inner and outer winner. While it was easy to be an inner winner with weekly planning, mission of making the public issue a success and proactively working with a winner's mindset, the challenging part was to be an outer winner. In each of his interactions with various people regarding the IPO, Dev reminded himself and applied the key elements of empathy and social skills. He focused on communication, influence, persuasion and overcoming objections.

While at his job, Dev reminded himself — *Any interview, any meeting, any conference creates tension and anxiety in us. This tension stunts our thinking. With the result that though you know a lot about the subject, you fail to bring forth effectively. The question is how to avoid the stress? Think and feel that you are speaking to the divinity in the other person. Sometimes the other person might unnerve you. But once you see the divinity in the other person and recognize that we are all children of the same God, it will not bother you.* The act of seeing divinity in the other person helped Dev to work on his empathy and social skills.

He worked for the success of the project and hardly thought of the personal rewards. He gave his best. What mattered to Dev was the success of the project and not his personal comfort. With small wins at different milestones in the project, Dev got the self-motivation he needed. With the right space and freedom provided by his boss, Dev felt driven to make things happen.

Whenever the going got tough on the project, Dev said to himself: *what is life without problems? Don't arrive at a decision till you have considered the problem in its totality. Base your decisions on strength, righteousness and not on weakness, fear and personal considerations. Go out of your way to help others and don't expect anything in return.*

Movies like *The Ten Commandments* and *Ben-Hur* inspired him. Travails of Moses and Ben Hur, where the heroes fought against all odds and kept their human spirit inching forward, gave Dev strength to work during difficult times.

Behind the success of the project, there was one unknown person. Only Dev knew it in his heart. This person was someone Dev befriended when he was in Mumbai. This person had visited Dev's office in Bangalore and the subsequent interaction gave Dev the idea for the brilliant financial structuring of the public issue. While the financial associate in question may not have known the knowledge and the trigger he had passed on to Dev, it was Dev and Dev alone who knew the profound impact of that thirty-minute interaction. Some may call it luck. To this day, Dev silently remembers him and thanks him because his life and career had transformed that day and had set him up for an upward spiral. That big day happened almost seven years after his B-school graduation.

Dev once again witnessed and experienced the operation of challenge, willingness and support in his life. He accepted the challenge of making the public issue succeed. He was willing to do it and maybe that stemmed from his previous experience in the capital markets and his competencies in that area. He got the right support from his boss. When all these three ingredients of challenge, willingness and support fell in place, the outcome was positive.

The One-minute Manager

In his day-to-day work and interactions with his team, Dev found it very useful to apply the three principles of *The One-Minute*

Manager, a profound book written by Dr. Spencer Johnson and Ken Blanchard. The three principles pertained to one minute goal setting, one minute praise and one minute reprimand.

	ONE-MINUTE MANAGER
Step 1	Goal setting
Step 2 (a)	Praise OR
Step 2 (b)	Reprimand
Step 3	Back to Step 1

The three principles pertained to one minute goal setting, one minute praise and one minute reprimand.

As Dev worked on projects, he tried to motivate his team members by setting goals. As the team members performed their tasks, Dev observed their behaviour and on satisfactory progress, he praised them. In difficult situations, where the team members were not doing satisfactory work, Dev asked himself whether it was a capability problem or a willingness problem. Where it was the former, he trained and guided them, and reset the goals. Where it was a willingness problem, he counseled them. He avoided delivering a reprimand as much as possible, unless pushed to his limits. And when he did it, Dev admonished the behaviour and reminded the team member that he was fine as a person, but it was his behaviour that needed correction. He kept the difference between the person and his behaviour in mind while pointing out mistakes to a team member.

Building Trust

Building trust and becoming trustworthy are two key elements of becoming an outer winner. Dev asked himself, *how do I build trust with my team members?*

> **Building trust and becoming trustworthy are two key elements of becoming an outer winner.**

The answer unfolded as follows: *I build trust by keeping my promises, by keeping my commitments, by sincerely respecting and most important, by not speaking ill about a team member behind his back. Many a time, I do make a mistake of unconsciously commenting about a team member in his absence. This may cause other team members to lose trust in me, because they may infer that I do the same with them in their absence.*

This point is so crucial that many a time we lose sight of it. It is very important to note and keep in mind to respect the absentee. RESPECT, RESPECT, RESPECT is the key. When you respect another person, everything else follows. You keep your promises and commitments to the other person. There may be times when it may not be possible to honor a commitment by a particular timeline. In such instances, it will help to proactively get back to the other person and communicate the same. Explain the circumstances of the case and recommit to a new timeline.

By building trust, you become trustworthy. And with trust comes cooperation. And with both higher trust and higher cooperation come higher levels of communication. Imagine the kind of teamwork that you would have with a communication that is supported by the two pillars of trust (openness) and cooperation. That kind of teamwork would produce amazing results and outcomes. Stephen Covey beautifully illustrates this concept in his book on *The 7 Habits of Highly Successful People* as below.

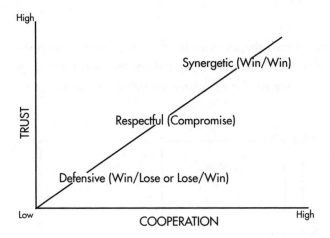

Thinking Win-win

Dev told himself — *To achieve still superior levels of teamwork, you need in each team member the quality of thinking win-win. You play not only for yourself but for the team. To understand this more, you need to have courage and consideration. At times, you need to let go and give consideration to the other team member so that your team can win the game. At other times, you need to show courage and shoulder the responsibilities when the other team members are falling like nine pins (say like in the game of cricket) so that your team still wins. It is the genius of courage AND consideration. It is the genius of AND and not the paradigm of OR. It is not courage OR consideration. It is 'AND'. Sometimes I play courageously AND do so with a feeling of consideration. At other times, I play considerately (down play)*

AND do so with a feeling of courageousness. No one knows it best than me.

I hope you, the reader, get that! Falling back on Covey, the concept is diagrammatically shown below.

To achieve still superior levels of teamwork, you need in each team member the quality of thinking win-win. It is the genius of courage AND consideration.

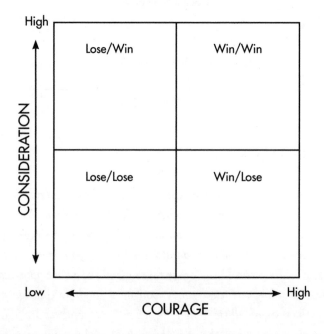

In one of the team meetings, Dev explained the concept of Win-Win by showing the picture of the two donkeys as illustrated below. Initially, the two donkeys are pulling against each other as each one wanted to eat the grass on its side, to meet its own self-interest. But the two head nowhere. Then they turn around to discuss and the wisdom dawns on them that should they think win-win, there is enough for both of them to share, eat and meet their mutual interests. This is so important. Life is not always zero sum game where we work on win-lose. Life is about keeping a positive outlook and coming up with creative solutions through a win-win scenario. Behind the cornerstones of courage and consideration is the presence of an abundant mentality. That there is enough for everyone and that life is all about living and letting live, that life is about empathy.

Life is about positive sum game and coming up with creative solutions through win-win.

Abundant Mentality

Abundant mentality means not to have a crab mentality. You would have seen that in a big jar of crabs, when a particular crab makes an attempt to get out of the jar, the others pull it down. Most often, most people behave in this way. It is only when a person conquers himself, develops a big heart and becomes appreciative of others, that he starts moving towards developing an abundant mentality. He sees himself in others and enjoys the achievements of others without belittling them. He feels no envy and jealousy. He rises above those negative feelings and applauds the achievements of others.

It is easy to fall in the trap of paucity mentality, which is a negation of abundant mentality. You need to be alert. Whenever such negative thoughts arise, you should be able to give yourself a whack on the head and turn the negative to positive. It is always easy to fall into the temptation of critiquing for no reason and belittling others. It is easy to spiral down the path of negativity. Paucity mentality, like gravity, pulls you down. It requires huge effort to come up with positivity and abundant mentality, as you are going against a strong pull of negativity. It is important that to move towards the path of leadership, you need to turn 180 degrees from paucity mentality to abundant mentality. This is a continuous work in progress in life.

> It is easy to fall in the trap of paucity mentality, which is a negation of abundant mentality.

Every day in our lives, there is a battle raging within us, like the Kurukshetra war in the *Mahabharata*, the war of the good against the bad. Which one will *you* allow to win? If you are strong, *you* will allow the good to win. If you are weak, *you* will allow the bad to win. The choice is yours!

The *choice* is indeed *yours*! Gandhi named his autobiography *My Experiments with Truth*. Every day, *you* need to exercise your *choice* to be 'with truth' or 'against truth'! One's journey in life is about realizing the Truth! Swami Vivekananda in his writings interprets truth beautifully by saying, "That which makes you strong is Truth and that which makes you weak is Untruth."

Therefore, if the whole of life's journey is about realizing the Truth, then it means that it is all about becoming strong – mentally, spiritually and socially. It is easy to be strong mentally and spiritually in isolation by negating society and moving away to an ashram. It is not that easy to be strong mentally and spiritually while living and interacting in society, without escaping to an ashram. That is the challenge, yours and mine! Gandhi demonstrated it. He had shown us the way. He was therefore called *Mahatma* (Great Soul) by none other than the Nobel Laureate Rabindranath Tagore.

Around this time, Dev watched the film *Gandhi*. The movie taught him lessons in leadership and teamwork. Below is the narrative of the film collected from various blogs and articles with the idea that the story may provide some glimpses to the concept of inner winner and outer winner.

Richard Attenborough's Oscar-winning film *Gandhi*, released in 1982, is a biopic on the life of Mohandas Gandhi.

The film begins with the assassination of Gandhi on January 30, 1948. After the evening prayers, Gandhi begins his walk. Nathuram Godse, his assassin, shoots him in the chest. Gandhi exclaims, "Hey Ram!" ("Oh God!"), and then falls

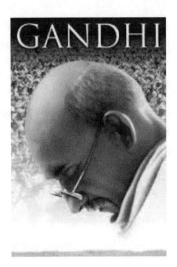 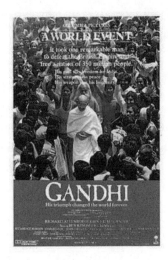

dead. The film continues with his funeral procession, attended by dignitaries from around the world.

Gandhi is portrayed as a man of profound simplicity. The story goes back to South Africa in 1893, when apartheid was at its peak. Mohandas Gandhi (Ben Kingsley), who finished his graduation in England, is not aware of this fact while traveling by train with a first-class ticket. A guard throws Gandhi out of the train for being a non-white and that action results in a sudden awakening for Gandhi.

Daunted by such injustice, ranting against the system, Gandhi feels he has no choice but protest. His words fail and Gandhi uses direct action, burning his identity card in front of the police. His subsequent arrest flashes as headlines and captures the attention of the whole world. Finally, the government recognizes some rights for Indians.

After this victory, Gandhi is back in India, where he is considered a national hero. It urges him to continue the struggle for India's independence from the British Empire. He mounts a campaign of non-violent non-cooperation on an unprecedented scale, coordinating millions of Indians.

Dev watched the film closely several times. He could appreciate and see the concept of inner winner and outer winner coming out alive! Reading and seeing inspirational stories from the perspective of concepts, theories and frameworks reinforced his understanding of leadership. He could relate to the elements of winner's mindset — being proactive, trust, teamwork and leadership.

During the 90s, as Dev kept growing in the corporate world with increased responsibilities, India witnessed the assassination of Rajiv Gandhi. In 1991, the Liberation Tigers of Tamil Eelam's (LTTE) suicide bomber blew up the prime minister of India during the pre-general election campaign. The same year, Narasimha Rao took over as the prime minster and master-minded the economic reforms program.

As Dev built his career, his son was born. Dev's father retired from the public hospital in his home town, Hyderabad. Now and then he visited Dev in Bangalore and spent time with his grandson. He initiated his grandson into writing the first letters. Rewards came in for Dev in the form of a car and other amenities. He was able to take his parents for outing in his own new car. One day, Dev asked himself about his plans for the future. His son was growing up and he wanted to provide a steady education at one place without the anxiety of moving from city to city because of job transfers. Dev got a break in the form of a new job and moved from Bangalore to Hyderabad. He experienced the joy of being with his parents and looked forward to the silent support of his family as he continued working hard in his career. At the same time, Dev wanted to do those little things for his father which he otherwise could not have done living in a faraway city.

In the five years leading to the year 2000 (Y2K), there were several landmark events in the country. In 1995, West Bengal Chief Minister Jyoti Basu made the first call from Kolkata to inaugurate the cellular services in India. In 1996, the Congress Party suffered the worst ever electoral defeat as BJP emerged as the largest single party. In 1998, BJP formed the coalition government under Prime Minister Atal Bihari Vajpayee. India carried out more nuclear tests, leading to widespread international condemnation. In 1999, Vajpayee made the historic bus trip to Pakistan to meet Prime Minister Nawaz Sharif to sign a bilateral peace declaration. In 1999, tensions in Kashmir led to an altercation with Pakistan in the icy heights around Kargil and India won the battle. Y2K also saw the rise of the Indian IT sector.

Key Points

To become an outer winner, you need to work on six things (1) Empathy (2) Social skills (3) Principles of one-minute manager (4) Trust (5) Thinking win-win (6) Abundant mentality

This chapter is the second step in transforming your life.

Action Points for You

1. Practice empathy. Making an effort to understand the other person's perspectives and feelings.

2. Hone social skills that involve communication, influence

and resolving conflicts.

3. Become a one-minute manager with goal setting, praise and reprimand.

4. Build trust. At the root of it is learning to keep promises and genuinely respecting another individual.

5. Think win-win. Creative problem-solving and coming up with a third alternative so that you win and the other person wins, too.

6. Practice abundance.

7. Remember that all the above points are work-in-progress and there is no end to perfection.

8. Read biographies/autobiographies of people whom you admire and see as role models.

9. Watch films listed in the appendix from a management perspective of leadership and team work.

CHAPTER | **4**

Problem Solving

We can't solve problems by using the same kind of thinking we used when we created them.

— Albert Einstein

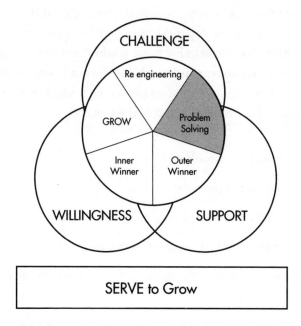

Like a doctor solving medical ailments, a manager solves organizational ailments. Is there a generic or heuristic method to solving ailments or problems?

Problems are so varied in nature. Like a human body has various organs and associated systems, like heart (cardiovascular), lungs (pulmonary), stomach (gastro), bones (orthopedics), etc., so does an organization with various departments and associated systems, like marketing, finance, operations, human resources, etc. Problems can arise in any of the departments. An organization can face problems in marketing, finances, operations, human resources, etc., and MBA as a discipline has developed over the years to address these problems and challenges. The designation of manager exists because organizational problems exist, too. If there are no problems, where is the need for managers?

Applied Knowledge Helps Solving Problems

While as a management professional, Dev acquired the technical knowledge to address organizational problems in various areas, the question that arose in his mind is whether there is a generic way or steps that one can use to achieve the same results. Through reading and search, Dev did come across a seven-step generic method to solve problems. Here is the method:

Step 1: Identify the problem

Step 2: Analyze the problem

Step 3: Identify the root cause

Step 4: Come up with alternative solutions

Step 5: Do a cost benefit analysis for each of the alternative solutions

Step 6: Pick up the best alternative solution and implement

Step 7: Review

The seven-step algorithm was enough for Dev to make sense of complex problems and provide the necessary direction to the group to solve any issue that cropped up at work. Dev dubbed it as 'solution oriented thinking'. The trick lies in recalling, remembering and applying the steps for the problem at hand. Many a time, as a manager, Dev realized that he did forget occasionally to remember and implement these simple seven steps. In such instances, he got poor outcomes. Dev also noted that the method can be applied not only to solve organizational problems but also personal issues.

Dev came across a seven-step generic method to solve problems.

In the first step, identifying the problem is the PROBLEM. Here one may need to define the boundaries and scope of the problem. One may take the help of powerful frameworks like the Porter's Five Forces and PEST (political, economic, social and technological) to arrive at the scoping of the problem.

In the second step, a useful technique is the cause-effect diagram (source: tipqc.org) also known as the Fishbone Diagram. In the diagram below, different causes (like methods, materials, equipment, people and environment) lead to the effect (or problem),i.e., CLABSI.

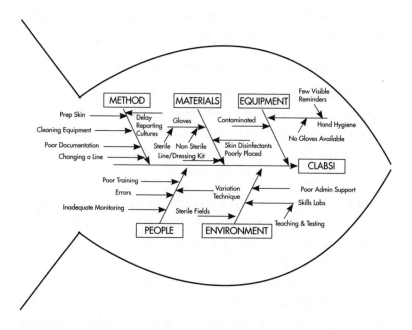

In the third step, through the effort of data collection, one may discern that 20 percent of the above factors would be leading to 80 percent of the problem (known as Pareto Analysis). For simplicity, one may discern in the above example that poor METHODS is the root cause for the problem. Data collection may show that evidence and therefore the inference. The root cause may not be the materials, equipment, people and environment.

In the fourth step, one comes up with alternative solutions through brainstorming techniques. Here freewheeling and creativity is exercised initially looking at possibilities without judgment. Later constraints and conditions are imposed to arrive at feasible solutions.

In the fifth step, one accounts for the cost and looks at the benefits.

In the sixth step, understanding the benefits, one arrives at the best solution with minimum cost.

In the final step, one implements and reviews.

Besides the seven-step problem solving, Dev picked up other management tools by doing a thorough study on the subject of Project Management and Total Quality Management (TQM). Some of the TQM tools that caught Dev's attention were PDCA (Plan, Do, Check and Act), Six Sigma, etc.

All these tools hint at one important point. They are simple. They spring from common sense. They are laced with wisdom. These tools are not rocket science. But the ability to remember the tools (the rules, the sequence of steps, heuristics) and applying the tools calls for high level of DISCIPLINE. Please note that DISCIPLINE cannot be taught in any MBA program. It has to be caught. It has to be acquired, assimilated and practiced. DISCIPLINE springs from perseverance and patience. When one applies the tools repeatedly, he attains mastery. And it takes more than 10,000 hours of practice to attain mastery and become a subject matter expert as mentioned by Malcolm Gladwell in his book *Outliers*.

Dev also realized that one should have FAITH in the tools. FAITH unfolds from purity, purpose and intent. With repeated application based on FAITH, accompanied by hits and misses, one hones the skill and moves towards the path of perfection!

DISCIPLINE and FAITH are what really matters in the repeated application of tools in solving problems and achieving successful outcomes.

At work, Dev told himself that as a manager he has to enjoy solving problems. While writing his journal, he penned: *When I confront a problem, I have to solve it like a doctor – diagnose the problem with the help of management tools. When I go to office, let me not forget to take my management tools along. These tools have a tendency to get rusted. So keep oiling them whenever required. Unless you keep using these tools, you will never become an expert. Therefore, conscious practice is needed. In the process, I move from unconscious incompetence to conscious incompetence to conscious competence to unconscious competence.*"

Most of the times in an organization, problem-solving is not done in isolation. A whole group is involved and it is very important that one develops the ability to facilitate a discussion. Sometimes one is involved in building a system from scratch and at other times one has to work on improving the existing system. Dev told himself that —*When I build a system, I will extend my analytical thinking to cover all the loopholes; when I confront a system, I will see how I can improve upon it. I will not ignore or overlook intuitive thoughts that may come from within me or from others. Let me take them up and explore. Let me think and think all the time. To do so, let me precede the thinking with the WHY spirit.*

During problem-solving, controversies arise. During a disagreement, the instant we feel anger, we cease to strive for the truth and begin striving for ourselves. Dev on reflection told himself: *Most of the time, any meeting, any interview or any conference overawes us. As a result, tension is created that stunts our thinking. In the process, though I know a lot about the subject, I fail to make my articulation effective. The question is how to avoid the tension? Probably the trick lies in thinking and feeling that I am speaking to the divinity in the other person. Sometimes the other person might unnerve me. But once I see the divinity in the other person and recognize that we are all part of the same Divine, it will not bother me.* It is very important to develop a calm and steady mind. Realize that we are attacking the problem and not the person across the table to find the solution. We need to develop the knack for separating the problem from the person.

The Next Five Years

One of the most memorable incidents in Dev's life was when his father seeded the idea of the whole family going on a Golden Triangle trip to North India, covering Agra, Jaipur and Delhi. His father sponsored the trip entirely, but he left the entire planning and execution to Dev, who put the problem-solving steps and project management tools to good use at that time. Everyone chipped in and made the trip a grand success. It was indeed an incredible experience for Dev and the entire family.

Dev started teaching as a visiting faculty at one of the local business schools. One of the subjects that he taught was the Theory of Constraints by Eliyahu Goldratt, his favourite. And one of his beloved books that he recommended others to read was

Goal, again written by Goldratt. The book provided a signature method of identifying constraints and removing constraints to solve problems.

Life is one continuous problem-solving exercise. At different stages of our life, only the nature of problems changes. We have problems as adolescents, as students, as a married person, as a parent, as a retired person and ultimately the trouble of ageing gracefully! Solving these problems with a smile on the face like Lord Krishna is the journey that we need to make in life.

Key Points

Become a problem-solver by adopting the seven-step method

Step 1: Identify the problem

Step 2: Analyze the problem

Step 3: Identify the root cause

Step 4: Come up with alternative solutions

Step 5: Do a cost benefit analysis for each of the alternative solutions

Step 6: Pick up the best and implement

Step 7: Review

This chapter on 'Problem solving' is the third step to transform your life.

Action Points for You

Practice the seven-step method

CHAPTER | 5

Reengineering Yourself

Success consists of going from failure to failure without loss of enthusiasm.

– Winston Churchill

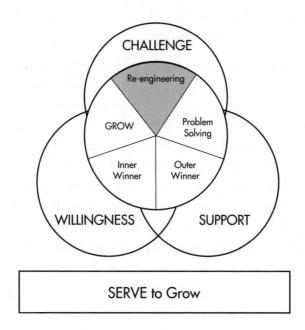

By the time he reached late thirties, Dev realized that to bring change, he needed to reengineer himself. This meant becoming an inner winner and an outer winner. It is leading self, leading others and within that context to have the ability to solve problems to bring forth positive results.

Which comes first? Being an inner winner or being an outer winner? The answer is clear — it is being an inner winner. Several examples flashed inside Dev's mind to support this precept.

For example, Sachin Tendulkar's mastery on batting is a reflection of his achievement that led to his getting the Bharat Ratna Award. As an individual, he is very authentic. He means what he says and there is no duplicity. These two qualities of achievement and authenticity is an inspiration to millions of people. He has a huge fan following and is seen as role model. He has made every Indian feel proud with his unbelievable feats and dream run in the game of cricket.

We come across many a person who has deep respect for the tough teacher when one was a student. The toughness from the teacher helped one to doubly work hard and learn. One cherishes and values that learning and owes it to one's demanding teacher. At times, one might hate the teacher but realizes that it has helped in one's personal development. So what are the attributes of the teacher that stand out first that make him to be remembered. The teacher pushes for excellence in his student. The teacher may not relate, be affable or socialize with his student. The teacher demands excellence out of himself and his student and values the path of being an inner winner first.

So the case rests. Focus on the inner winner first. The outer winner naturally follows. When Tendulkar excels, he becomes a role model. People around emulate him. People see other qualities of Tendulkar, i.e., humility, supporting nature, etc., and emulate such winning habits as followers. That emulation by others is what makes Sachin Tendulkar into an outer winner.

Amitabh Bachchan, a Bollywood icon and a deeply respected figure in the Indian cinema, had this to say on Sachin at the time of the latter's farewell from cricket: "At an age when we were struggling to button up our trousers, this young lad was facing the fiercest bowling attacks ever seen in the realm of the game and coming out victorious!" Both Sachin Tendulkar and Amitabh Bachchan got elected into the list of 25 greatest global living legends in a poll conducted in December 2013 by NDTV in celebration of its 25 years of successful completion as a TV news channel. Tendulkar received the highest civilian award, the Bharat Ratna, on the day of his retirement from cricket in November 2013. Bachchan was bestowed with the Padma Vibhushan in 2016.

You are clever when you change the world (outer winner), but you are wise when you change yourself (inner winner). Inner winner scores over the outer winner when it comes to the question which element is first!

Which comes first? Being an inner winner or being an outer winner? The answer is clear — it is being an inner winner.

In his career spanning over a decade and a half, Dev moved from an individual contributor to a general manager. In making the transitions, the tools of inner winner and outer winner helped him substantially. All along, he kept learning, crafting and honing his skills on building bonds, collaboration, cooperation and leveraging diversity.

As Dev continued to keep reading and reflecting, he mapped and correlated the understanding from different sources on the subject in a pattern as below. For instance, when he read R. Gopalakrishnan's book *What the CEO Really Wants from You* based on his 40 years of experience in the corporate world, he immediately sought its relevance within his framework of inner and outer winner. Gopalakrishnan is a respected leader and works with the Tata Group as one of its board of directors.

	DISC PROFILE	INSTRUMENT	R. GOPALAKRISHNAN'S BOOK
Inner	Dominance	Director	Achievement
Outer	Influence	Socializer	Advocacy
Outer	Steadiness	Relator	Affability
Inner	Conscientiousness	Thinker	Authentic

Dev was clear that he should not get lost in semantics and jargon. Therefore the effort to make notes, map those notes to his earlier readings on the subject, helped a deeper understanding. This in turn provided the direction for enhanced application of the learning.

As mentioned earlier in the third chapter, Dev found it very useful to apply the three principles of One-Minute Manager pertaining to one-minute goal setting, one-minute praise and one-minute reprimand. However, he noted that he may have to deliver different styles for different behaviours of his team mates. His reading and understanding of *Situational Leadership* by Ken Blanchard and Paul Hersey was a very big value-add to his leadership development capability.

What is situational leadership? When it should be applied and how it should be applied?

In the situational leadership model, there are four styles that a leader can deliver matching to different stages of group development for effective outcomes.

Dev could not help but appreciate relating this model to his experience of teaching his seven-year-old son cycling. Though he was not aware of the model at the time, he awakened to the fact

LEADERSHIP STYLE		STAGE OF GROUP DEVELOPMENT		
S 1	High Directive and Low Supportive Behaviour	**Directing**	GDS 1	Productivity (Competence) is Low	Morale (Commitment) is High
S 2	High Directive and High Supportive Behaviour	**Coaching**	GDS 2	Productivity (Competence) is Average	Morale (Commitment) is Low
S 3	Low Directive and High Supportive Behaviour	**Supporting**	GDS 3	Productivity (Competence) is above average	Morale (Commitment) is average
S 4	Low Directive and Low Supportive Behaviour	**Delegating**	GDS 4	Productivity (Competence) is High	Morale (Commitment) is High

that for his son to have successfully picked up the skill of cycling, he in fact had delivered the four leadership styles as described above.

Dev recalled the bright Sunday morning when his enthusiastic son came to him with his new cycle, eager to learn to ride it. Dev taught his son the fundamentals of the bicycle, the functions of the pedal, the clutch and the brake. He demonstrated how to get on to the bike and ride (Dev used the Directing Style – high directive and low supportive behaviour). Next he asked his son to get on to the bike and pedal while he held the bicycle seat. As hours passed and as his son's skill picked up, Dev started distancing himself from holding the bicycle seat. He could see that his son kept pedaling on his own, but when he realized that his dad was not nearby, he panicked, which resulted in the boy losing control and falling down. Dev once again held the bicycle seat and as his son cycled, he kept distancing himself from the bicycle. But his son still kept falling down. Slowly, the boy lost his morale. But Dev remained supportive. He motivated him and built confidence in the boy by saying that at his age, Dev himself fell down many times (Dev here used the Coaching Style – high directive and high supportive behaviour).

The next week around, the father-son duo once again came back to the bicycling track. The competence of his son in cycling improved substantially. Dev reduced the level of giving instructions while at the same time kept his son motivated with encouraging words (Dev used the Supporting Style – low directive and highly supportive behaviour).

Then one Sunday, Dev's son started cycling on his own without his father's help. Dev reckoned that his son had learned the method of cycling and become confident. His son was riding the bicycle with high competence and morale. He left his son on his own, only occasionally checking to make sure that he is doing fine (Dev used the Delegating Style – low directive and low supportive behaviour).

> In the situational leadership model, there are four styles that a leader can deliver matching to different stages of group development for effective outcomes.

The essence of situational leadership model is 'Different strokes for different folks'. Different strokes refer to different leadership styles. Different folks refer to different stages of group's development or individual's development. To expand the rule further, it is 'Different strokes for different folks at around the same time,' as well as 'Different strokes to the same individual at different times'.

This model works!

Dev could see continuous opportunities for applying this model at work for his team's development. The more he used it, the better were the outcomes. He diagnosed the group better and therefore prescribed and delivered the style that suited that stage. At times, he erred in the diagnosis and therefore it did not produce the desired results. With time and practice, he became adept at this and produced desired outcomes consistently. It is all about practice, practice and practice. Practice makes a man perfect!

It was then that he started having faith in the situational leadership tool. Dev started sharing the advantages of this tool with other team leaders in his organization so that they could

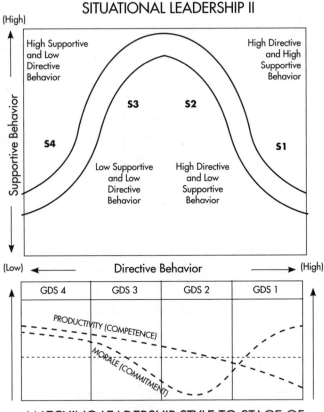

SITUATIONAL LEADERSHIP II

MATCHING LEADERSHIP STYLE TO STAGE OF GROUP DEVELOPMENT

also produce better results. He taught them when it made sense to spend time with the subordinate and when to let go.

This style of leadership with continuous diagnosis helped Dev empower his team members. It is like, at the low end of the continuum, you feed a starving man fish one day, you feed him for that day only. At the high end of the continuum, if you teach the same man to fish, you are empowering him for life.

LOW	MEDIUM	HIGH
Nurturing	Equipping	Developing
Caring	Training for work	Training for personal growth
Helping	Teaching	Mentoring
Establishing	Releasing	Empowering
Short term	Medium term	Long term
Relational	Transactional	Transformational

Dev noted that underlying the movement to the high end of empowering is the social competence of Empathy. It is all about the needs, awareness and concern for other people's feelings.

Teams go through four stages: Forming, Storming, Norming and Performing. It is the leader of the team who inspires and guides the other members to move from one stage to another. The leader acts as the catalyst, initiating and managing the change. He nurtures the relationships, collaborates the necessities and establishes cooperation between the team members. He creates the synergy in pursuing collective goals and thus builds team capabilities.

In a team, there are different people with different perspectives. A leader recognizes this diversity. He values these differences and facilitates the team to come up with creative alternatives and solutions. The leader de-escalates disagreements and orchestrates resolutions. The process that makes this happen is nothing but synergy. Synergy is the process that reveals the third alternative or win-win solution. A true leader always recognizes opportunities for synergy and motivates the team to find a win-win solution.

In the diagram below, taken from Stephen Covey's book on the concept of synergy, you move from the zone of conflict to the zone of synergy. In that zone, you narrow down the extreme positions taken by you and others. There is a mutual understanding of moving from a no-win to a win-win.

A true leader always recognizes opportunities for synergy and leverages the differences towards finding the third alternative.

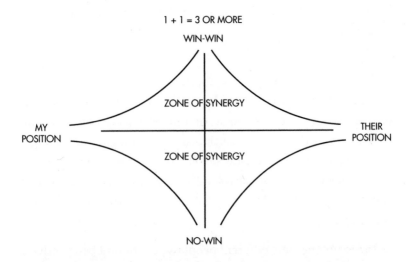

Understand that to reach a win-win situation through the synergy process, one needs to recognize the importance of having an 'abundant mentality'. To win friends and influence people, one surely needs certain persuasive tactics. But to be persuasive, one need to understand and empathize with others and that only comes from a place of feeling abundant from within.

While at work, Dev reminded himself: *every day is a day of competition. The meaning of competition should not be viewed in a negative sense. I run my race. I self-actualize myself through work. My work is an offering and dedication to God. At the same time, I keep my eyes open. I can learn quite a few things from my peers to better my work. Look at it this way – God is giving you an opportunity to see for yourself how you can perform better. Seeing others do better than you should not demotivate you or create unhealthy tension. When someone else excels, it is God's way of motivating you, inspiring you.*

The idea of competition spurred Dev to re-engineer himself, lead with a compelling vision, collaborate with all team members and establish internal cooperation to pursue collective goals.

Looking back over the last 18 years of his professional life, Dev reminded himself of the notes that he had made at the start of his career. *"At the workplace, come up with a clear objective – prioritizing; maximum result and minimum effort. Concentrate on subordinates and peers, and observe superiors; delegate work; get fresh ideas and develop new thinking with the help of books, newspaper articles, etc.; don't waste time as it is scarce. Even when forced to go to a movie knowing it would be a waste of time, use the time to plan your next step in personal life or at work; Keep yourself physically fit. Your thinking is absolutely clear when you are healthy. When you are not, don't take life-altering decisions."*

Dev also noticed that he had written 10 rules for himself that should guide his work life based on experiences and reflections of his post-graduate college life. And they were:

1. Strive for perfection and realize God. Many a times it may appear that you don't have enough work. When that thought comes, plan and create new work.

2. Be emotionally strong. Don't let people's comparisons and comments affect you.

3. If you find a better person, he is not your competitor. View him as your role model.

4. If the other person has ego, let that not bother you, for it is the devil at work.

5. Be fearless (the word *abhaya* in Upanishads).

6. In spite of your weaknesses, always speak positively about yourself.

7. Be 100 percent optimistic.

8. Keep good health.

9. There is no greater joy than hard work. Be focused.

10. Your family is everything.

Dev had also written in his notes to regularly write a resume. *"Write a resume (300 words) on your outstanding achievements. Write resumes on your subordinates. Make an effort to understand the people who influence your career. With peers, overestimate your faults. With subordinates, underestimate your virtues. Understand the goals and objectives of your reporting officer and also that of the reviewing officer,"* his note read.

In his day-to-day work and interactions with his team, Dev reflected and noted how he found it very useful to apply the principles of One-Minute Manager, Situational Leadership and Team Synergy.

Dev also noted and synthesized the five key elements of EMOTIONAL INTELLIGENCE (diagram in the third chapter) in the tables below:

SELF-AWARENESS	SELF-MANAGEMENT	SOCIAL AWARENESS	SOCIAL SKILL
Emotional self-awareness: The ability to read and understand your emotions as well as recognize their impact on work performance, relationships and the like. **Accurate self-assessment:** A realistic evaluation of your strengths and limitations. **Self-confidence:** A strong and positive sense of self-worth.	**Self-control:** The ability to keep disruptive emotions and impulses under control. **Trustworthiness:** a consistent display of honesty and integrity. **Conscientiousness:** the ability to manage yourself and your responsibilities. **Adaptability:** Skill at adjusting to changing situations and overcoming obstacles. **Achievement orientation (Motivation):** The drive to meet and internal standard of excellence. **Initiative:** A readiness to seize opportunities.	**Empathy:** Skills at sensing other people's emotions understanding the irrespective, and taking an active interest in their concerns. **Organizational awareness:** The ability to read the currents of organizational life, build decision networks, E1 **Service orientation:** The ability to recognize and meet customers needs.	**Visionary leadership:** The ability to take charge and inspire with a compelling vision. **Influence:** The ability to wield a range of persuasive tactics. **Developing others:** The propensity to bolster the abilities of others through feedback and guidance. **Communication:** Skill at listening and at sending clear convincing, and well-tuned messages. **Change catalyst:** Proficiency in initiating new ideas and leading people in a new direction. **Conflict Management:** The ability to de-escalate disagreements and orchestrate resolutions. **Building bonds:** Proficiency at cultivating and maintaining a web of relationships. **Teamwork and collaboration:** competence at promoting cooperation and building teams.

Dev found it very useful to apply the principles of One-Minute Manager, Situational Leadership and Team Synergy.

Around this time, Dev watched the film *Lagaan* and once again, learnt the importance of leadership and teamwork.

The Movie *Lagaan* and Its Lessons

Story (Source: Wikipedia)

The movie *Lagaan* (High Taxes) is a story about Bhuvan (Aamir Khan) and his band of villagers from Champaran during the late nineteen century in the British India. Captain Andrew Russell (Paul Blackthorne), the commanding officer imposes high taxes on people to pay from the local villages. The villagers approach Raja Puran Singh (Kulbhushan Kharbanda) to help them to dissuade the British from the payment of tax because of the prolonged draught. The Raja tells them that he is helpless as he is also bound by the British law.

In that moment, Captain Russell throws a wager. He makes Bhuvan a deal: the villagers will play a cricket match with the British. If the villagers win, there will be no taxes for three years. If the British win, the taxes will be tripled. The captain believes that cricket is a game that can never be mastered by the villagers. Bhuvan accepts the wager. The villagers disagree with Bhuvan. But he points out that as such since they cannot pay the current tax, they have nothing to lose.

Bhuvan assembles and coaches five villagers who showed the skill required to play it. He tells them that the game is much like Gilli Danda, which is an ancient Indian game. He is helped by Russels' sister Elizabeth (Rachel ShelleY) who believes that her brother's deal is unfair and secretly teaches Bhuvan's team the pointers on cricket. Her closeness with Bhuvan disturbs Gauri (Gracy Singh), childhood friend of Bhuvan and also who is in love with him. There is a twist in the plot with Lakha (Yashpal Sharma) who wants Gauri for himself. He decides to act as a spy for Russell because he feels that if Bhuvan loses the game and therefore his face, he will have a better chance to win over Gauri.

As other members of the village are ill-treated by the British, they join the team as they realize that winning would mean freedom. Bhuvan also invites Kachra (Aditya Lokia), an "untouchable" whose crippled arm allows him to throw a spin. Through this, the villagers' bias towards Kachra is also eradicated.

The second half of the movie is the cricket match. Winning the toss, Captain Russell elects to bat and the British team puts up a strong score with Kachra proving ineffective to spin with the new ball. In addition, Lakha deliberately drops the catches to abet the British. When Elizabeth informs Bhuvan about Lakha, the villagers chase Lakha to kill him. It is Bhuvan who comes to

Lakha's rescue and gives him a chance to prove his loyalty to the village and redeem himself.

On the second day of the match, with Lakha's diving catch and Kachra's hat trick, the British batting collapses from a strong 300 for three wickets to 323. With the villagers play the innings, Bhuvan and Deva (a Sikh who played cricket when he was a British Sepoy) provide a strong start. Deva misses out on his half century while Lakha gets hit on his head by a bouncer and falls on his stumps. Ismail (Raj Zutshi), a good batsman, leaves the game when hit on the leg.

On the third and final day, while other batsmen fall, Bhuvan scores his century. With Ismail returning, he scores more than a half century. The British unethically run out the runner and the game reduces to the last over with Kachra coming on to bat. With five runs to win the match and aided by a no ball by the British bowler in the last over, Bhuvan gets the chance to strike the last ball for a six. The ball is caught by Captain Russell but his feet are beyond the boundary line, resulting in the win of Bhuvan and his team.

Captain Russell is deposed from the cantonment by the Crown and the cantonment is disbanded. He is penalized to pay the uncollected tax. Elizabeth returns to England realizing that Bhuvan belongs to Gauri.

Eleven Key Lessons

The set of eleven lessons discussed below will help in the development of an ethical leadership that is critical for companies today (Source: Global Edge Software Ltd. and Wikipedia)

Lesson 1: Think of challenges as opportunities

When Captain Russell challenges Bhuvan to a game of cricket, Bhuvan accepts it because he knows that there is really no other option. It is a risk, but without taking risks, there are no rewards. Given the state of the Champaner region with no impending rains, Bhuvan viewed the choice of trying to reduce the "double tax" as a non-option against the possibility of a "10x" improvement in quality of life offered by a victory.

> In our lives too, we face challenges. We need to see them as opportunities for innovation.

Lesson 2: Envision and calibrate the goal

Once Bhuvan accepted the challenge, his vision was three years with no tax. It may have seemed unrealistic, but then that is what vision is made of. Visioning is about imagining a different future. Bhuvan not only envisioned big but also put devised a strategy to make that a reality.

To make things happen the way we want, we have to envision the future. You need to paint a picture of what we desire to achieve so that they get an idea too.

Lesson 3: Prioritize community before self

The important thing about Bhuvan's vision was that it was for the community, and not for himself. Neither in his speech nor in his action did Bhuvan put his interests before the village's. Bhuvan's vision of the greater good drew the support of the entire province.

Prioritize your company first. If your company succeeds,
you succeed.

Lesson 4:   Be determined in the face of resistance and opposition

This comes across many times in the movie. From the beginning,
when the entire village is against Bhuvan for taking up the
challenge to when the rest of his team refuses to play because
Bhuvan wants to include Kachra, an untouchable. In every
occasion, Bhuvan knows he is right. He stands up and answers
his critics with courage, winning their support in the end. We all
face these kinds of situation in our company at some stage or the
other.

Many a time, we give up and accept what we feel is
perhaps a lesser choice. It is at times like these that
we need to face up —as long as we know that we are
fighting for the right cause and not against a person.

Lesson 5:   Provide examples to step up understanding

Bhuvan simplified the challenge of learning cricket by portraying
it as something similar to *gilli-danda*. By doing this, he made the
impossible seem possible and made the insurmountable seem
probable. Metaphors have that effect and can be powerful in
helping transcend the seemingly unachievable.

As managers and leaders, we too have the task of
motivating our team to take up challenges in the
workplace. Vision needs to be broken down into a series
of activities that the team can understand, thus building a
pathway through the smog.

Lesson 6:   Make a Beginning

Bhuvan did not wait to begin. He did not look around. He made a
bat and a ball, got the child interested and began. Many times, we
worry too much and end up doing nothing. .

The only way one can test out new ideas is by taking
initiative and getting started. Only when we leave
the shore, will we see the vast blue ocean with its
opportunities unfolding.

Lesson 7:   Little victories are important at the start

The first time Bhuvan hits the ball, he did so in full view of the
public. He made it seem easy motivating them to participate. .

When starting any project, it is important to have small
wins at the beginning to motivate the team.

Lesson 8:   Provide support to the team members

Bhuvan stood for his people, even when they made mistakes. He
backed Kachra to the hilt and gave him a second chance (on the

second afternoon of the match) despite the pessimism of others.
He knew that Kachra can be a game changer. The confidence that
Bhuvan reposed in Kachra proved him right.

> It is vital that the captain supports his team, backing the
> right person at the right time for the right job.

Lesson 9:   Make the best use of the limited resources

Bhuvan depends on the rudimentary bat, ball and pads. He and
his team practiced at night with the entire village providing the
light through their torches. The villagers of Champaner had
limited resources, but they made the best use of them.

> You cannot always wait for the perfect tools or for the
> availability of right resources. As proactive managers,
> we must innovate —focus on getting the work done.
> When one has fewer resources, the mind and body
> persevere harder and more creatively.

Lesson 10:   Reposing Trust

Bhuvan had an abundant heart in pardoning Lakha, protecting
him from the wrath of the angry villagers and giving Lakha
another chance to prove his loyalty to the team. He earned the
trust of Lakha and this tilted the match in their favour.

Lesson 11:   Value based leadership

Bhuvan and his bunch of villagers lived for a goal bigger than themselves. They were selfless and stood for social justice by including Kachra, an untouchable into their team.

Lagaan received critical acclaim and awards, both in India as well as abroad. It became the third Indian film to be nominated for the Academy Award for Best Foreign Language Film after *Mother India* (1957) and *Salaam Bombay* (1988). It was one of the biggest box office hits of 2001.

The key secret behind re-engineering oneself is the sheer joy to be on the field like Sachin Tendulkar or in front of the camera like Amitabh Bachchan. This passion is very evident in their interviews, if one listens carefully. Actor Ajay Devgn mentioned in a reality show that one of the many things that he learnt from Bachchan was to be extremely enthusiastic or passionate for perfection to the work.

The other keys to re-engineering besides the passion are gratitude, learning from others and believing in oneself.

Another prominent actor, Shah Rukh Khan, mentioned the importance of gratitude in one's attitude and how tremendously lucky he had been all along while thanking God. He said that, as an actor, he will do anything that his audience would like. He emphasized the importance of hard work, the need to learn from everyone every day and never to take anything personally — that is, if rejected for a role, he takes it as if he is not apt for that role and has nothing to do with his abilities or talent. One needs to believe in oneself. It is critical that one does not get oneself subjected to other people's negative opinions. Oscar-winning music composer A.R. Rahman stresses on the ability to learn from everyone, including movie directors and other composers, as one of the reasons for his success.

The New Millennium

In 2001, Dev's father had to undergo a bypass surgery. Everyone in the family rushed forward to support him during this critical period. One of the things his father said at that time was, "While my elder son, a doctor, took care of my body, my younger son, Dev, looked after my spirit." Dev kept his old man's words close to his heart.

In 2002, Dev asked himself a key question: *what am I good at? What do I love doing? Can I make money out of that pursuit?*

Discover Your Calling

Dev discovered that he was happiest when he taught at the business school. Much against the wishes of his family and friends, Dev decided to follow his heart and took the plunge of teaching at a B-school. He read a lot, prepared hard for his sessions and started making a name for himself as a star faculty. Despite options given by his superior to be on the management side of the business school and earn a higher remuneration, Dev stuck to his decision of teaching and excelled at it. Dev went to spearhead the management development training programs for companies and faculty development training programs for colleges across the country. He also enrolled himself into a doctoral program.

Dev's father never questioned his son's career decisions. Instead, he silently acknowledged and supported his career moves. When in doubt, Dev would consult his father. His responses stemming from deep, philosophical insights and experience gave Dev answers regarding what to do next. Many a time, he used to remind Dev that whatever happens does happen for the good. His father used to tell Dev, "You may not perceive the hidden goodness in an apparently unpalatable event at a particular point of time, but will later appreciate the test that the higher power has put you through for your own good."

After his father's retirement in 2005, Dev made it a point to spend every Sunday evening with his parents. Dev enjoyed the discussions with his father during this time. The topics ranged from current events to history, religion and philosophy, and peppered with quick updates about the family.

In that same year, Dev got a big break. He got to head the learning and development facility of an MNC. Dev went on to hone his skills in education and training. He picked up great experience in leadership development efforts in his new organization and was instrumental in setting up a leadership development centre to train its local and international employees.

During the first decade of the 21st century, as Dev found his sweet spot in education and training, the country experienced great speed and momentum. In 2000, the US President Bill

Clinton made a groundbreaking visit to improve ties with India. The year marked the birth of India's billionth citizen. A high-powered rocket was launched by ISRO, adding India to the club of countries able to launch big satellites into space.

However, in 2001, massive earthquakes hit the western state of Gujarat, leaving at least 30,000 dead.

During that time, after over two years, Prime Minister Vajpayee met Pakistani President Pervez Musharraf at the historic Agra Summit. The meeting ended without a breakthrough or even a joint statement because of the differences over Kashmir.

In 2002, India and Pakistan amassed troops along the common border amid mounting fears of a looming war. India successfully test-fired a nuclear-capable ballistic missile, Agni, off its eastern coast. Retired scientist and the architect of India's missile program, Dr. A.P.J. Abdul Kalam, was elected President of India.

In 2004, there was a surprise victory for the Congress party in the general election. Dr. Manmohan Singh was sworn in as Prime Minister. India, along with Brazil, Germany and Japan, applied for a permanent seat on the UN Security Council. The year ended with the death of thousands when a tsunami, caused by an earthquake off the Indonesian coast, devastated coastal communities in South India and in the Andaman and Nicobar Islands.

In 2006, India's largest-ever rural jobs scheme was launched, aimed at lifting around 60 million families out of poverty. USA and India signed a nuclear agreement during the US President George W. Bush's visit to India. The US gave India access to civilian nuclear technology while India agreed to greater scrutiny for its nuclear program. In 2006, India's Mittal Steel acquired Arcelor for $34.3 billion to become the world's biggest steel maker, Arcelor Mittal, producing 10 percent of the world's steel.

In 2007, the government announced its strongest economic growth figures for 20 years — 9.4 percent. Economic liberalization in India in the 1990s and first decade of the 21st century had led to large changes in the economy. In January 2007, India's Tata Steel made a successful $11.3 billion offer to buy European steel maker Corus Group. The same year, Pratibha Patil became the first woman President of India.

Key Points

To re-engineer oneself, one needs to strengthen the dimensions of an inner and outer winner. One important skill in this process is the application of the situational leadership model while leading others within the context of solving problems to produce results and creating group synergy.

This chapter is the fourth step in transforming your life.

Action Points for You

1. Learn to apply situational leadership.

2. Leverage the group's diversity and creating group synergy.

3. Read the books listed in the appendix. Summarize points and reduce it to a mnemonic. Apply the learning.

4. Watch films listed in the appendix from a management perspective of leadership and team work.

5. Make it a point to listen to interviews of celebrities, successful businessmen, etc., on the TV.

The year 2008 was a significant one because that was the year Dev completed his PhD. He could see the pride in his parents' eyes. That same year, Dev's son joined a medical school.

By this time, Dev had become an accomplished trainer. His ratings were excellent and more and more people started attending his training programs.

Dev also made it a point to invest in himself by attending a few certification programs. One such program was Executive Coaching. It was five days long that created an impact on him. The essence of the training was to use the GROW Model (GROW is an acronym that stands for: Goal, Current Reality, Options (or Obstacles), Wrap-up (or Way Forward)) and observe the standards including maintaining confidentiality, being open without judgment, looking at the positives, listening and acknowledging.

During his five years in the field of training, Dev realized that while training made a 10 percent difference to the student, what really mattered was the follow-up coaching and the application of the principles taught during the training. This made up for the remaining 90 percent.

Dev went on to practice executive coaching and saw the transformation it could bring in the trainee. He saw for himself several cases where the transformation had happened. In one instance, a trainee who found it extremely difficult to get up in the morning and exercise began to do it all! In another instance, a trainee who found it difficult to get a job done from his subordinate could accomplish it! In many a case, the trainees reported increased productivity levels ranging from 25-75 percent.

It was with this faith that Dev started extolling the importance of executive coaching and how it can be used to unleash incredible performance from their team members. In one of his training sessions on executive coaching, Dev said, "The fundamental precept in executive coaching is that one does not advice. The trainee has the answers for himself and the job of the coach is to help the trainee find the answers through a process of Socrates Dialogue. Thus when the trainee discovers the answer, he owns it. During the dialogue, while the coach may have the answer ready for the trainee, the coach holds himself back from providing the same. This calls for immense patience from the coach. At every stage in the process, the coach works at heightening the awareness of the trainee and the options/choices that the trainee can exercise.

"Typically such a session may last for an hour, sometimes more and sometimes less. At the end of the session, the coach gives an assignment to do for the next week before they meet up again. Interactions of such nature take place week after week, for twelve weeks over a three-month period. Sometimes, based on the trainee's needs, it may stretch to six months."

Continuing with his explanation, Dev drew the diagram of the GROW Model below.

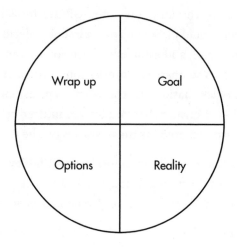

Dev explained that the GROW Model is a simple process for coaching and mentoring. He told his class that as a leader, one of their most important roles is to coach people under them to do their best. By doing this, they will be helping them make better decisions, solve problems that are holding them back, learn new skills, and otherwise progress their careers.

Some people are fortunate enough to get formal training in coaching. However, many people have to develop this important skill themselves. This may sound daunting. But if you equip yourself with some proven techniques, practice, and trust your instincts, you can become a great coach.

Referring to his notes that he made from www.mindtools. com, Dev said that the GROW Model is a simple yet powerful framework for structuring your coaching or mentoring sessions. Let us look at how to apply the model. GROW stands for: **G**oal, Current **R**eality, **O**ptions (or Obstacles), **W**rap up (or Way Forward).

A good way of thinking about the GROW Model is to think about how you would plan a journey. First, you decide where you are going (the goal), and establish where you currently are (your current reality).You then explore various routes (the options) towards your destination. In the final step, establishing your way forward, you ensure that you are committed to making the journey and are prepared for the obstacles on the way.

The model was originally developed in the 1980s by performance coach Sir John Whitmore, although other coaches, such as Alan Fine and Graham Alexander, have also helped to develop it.

In its traditional application, the GROW model assumes that the coach is not an expert in the "client's" situation. This means that the coach must act as a facilitator, helping the client select the best options, and not offering advice or direction.

When leaders coach their team members, or act as mentors to them, this may or may not apply. On one hand, it is more powerful for people to draw conclusions for themselves, rather than having these conclusions thrust upon them. On the other hand, as a team leader, you will often have expert knowledge to offer. Also, it is your job to guide your team members to make decisions that are best for your organization.

GROW stands for: Goal, Current Reality, Options (or Obstacles), Wrap up (or Way Forward).

To structure a coaching or mentoring session using the GROW model, take the following steps:

1. Establish the Goal

First, you and your team member need to look at the behaviour that you want to change and then structure this change as a *goal* that he wants to achieve. Make sure that this is a SMART goal — one that is Specific, Measurable, Attainable, Realistic and Time-bound. When doing this, it is useful to ask questions like:

a. How will you know that your team member has achieved this goal? How will you know that the problem or issue is solved?

b. Does this goal fit with his overall career objectives? And does it fit with the team's objectives?

2. Examine the Current Reality

Next, ask your team member to describe his current reality. This is an important step; too often, people try to solve a problem or reach a goal without fully considering their starting point, and often they are missing some information they need in order to reach their goal effectively. As your team member tells you about his current reality, the solution may start to emerge. Useful coaching questions at this step include the following:

a. What is happening now (what, who, when and how often)? What is the effect or result of this?

b. Have you (the team member) already taken any steps towards your goal?

c. Does this goal conflict with any other goals or objectives?

3. Explore the Options

Once you and your team member have explored the reality, it is time to determine what is possible – meaning all of the possible options for reaching his objective. Help your team member *brainstorm* as many options as possible. Then, discuss these and help him decide on the best ones. By all means, offer your own suggestions in this step. But let your team member offer his suggestions first and let him do most of the talking. It is important to guide in the right direction without actually making decisions for him. Typical questions that you can use to explore options are as follows:

a. What else could you do?

b. What if this or that constraint were removed?

c. Would that change things?

d. What are the advantages and disadvantages of each option?

e. What factors or considerations will you use to weigh the options?

f. What do you need to stop doing in order to achieve this goal?

g. What are the obstacles standing in your way?

4. Establish the Way Forward

By examining the current reality and exploring the options, your team member will now have a good idea of how he can achieve his goal. That is great, but in itself, this may not be enough. The final step is to get your team member to commit to specific actions in order to move forward towards his goal. In doing this, you will help him establish his will and boost his motivation. Useful questions to ask here include:

a. What will you do now, and when? What else will you do?

b. What could stop you moving forward? How will you overcome this?

c. How can you keep yourself motivated?

d. When do you need to review progress? Is it daily, weekly, monthly?

Finally, decide on a date when you will both review his progress. This will provide some accountability and allow him to change his approach if the original plan isn't working.

Dev further continued by saying that a great way to practice using the model is to address your own challenges and issues. By practicing on your own and getting yourself "unstuck," you will learn how to ask the most helpful questions. Then, write down some list of questions as prompts for future coaching sessions.

The two most important skills for a coach are the ability to *ask good questions* and the ability to *listen effectively*. Don't ask closed questions that call for a yes or no answer (such as, "Did that cause a problem?"). Instead, ask open-ended ones, like, "What effect did that have?" Be prepared with a list of questions for each stage of the GROW process. Use *active listening* skills and let your "client" do most of the talking. Remember that silence provides valuable thinking time: you don't always have to fill silence with the next question.

Giving an example, Dev cited an instance of helping a team member, Kapil, achieve his goals using the GROW model. "Kapil said that he would like a promotion to team leader within the next two years. This is a SMART goal – it's specific, measurable, attainable (as he already has one year of experience and there are several team leader positions in the department), relevant (both to Kapil's overall career aspirations and the team's mission) and time-bound.

Kapil and I looked at his current reality. He is in an entry-level position, but already has some of the skills needed to be team leader. I brainstormed the additional skills that he would need in order to be successful in a team leader role. He needed more experience in managing other people and dealing with overseas customers. He also needed to continue performing well in his role, so that he would be considered for a promotion when one is available.

Both of us then reviewed his options. To get the experience he needed, he could lead a small team on a small project. He could also spend time with the overseas team.

Finally, I established the way forward. I offered to let him lead a small team on a minor project. If he performed well, he could take on additional projects with more responsibility in the future. I agreed to review his progress in three months."

The acronym GROW stands for Goal, Reality, Options and Wrap-up as already mentioned earlier. In a session, the trainee picks up a problem or challenge that he is facing. He then sets a GOAL for himself. Through dialogue, the coach brings out awareness on the current REALITY of the situation and discusses the opportunities/threats and the strengths/weaknesses. The discussion leads to generation of OPTIONS/choices. By dwelling on the point of what serves best, the trainee makes a choice. The session ends with a WRAP-UP by the coach where a commitment from the trainee on the timeline is sought for the implementation of the goal.

During the dialogue, there are certain standards observed by the coach. To name the most important ones – keeping an open non-judgmental mind, refraining from giving advice, helping the trainee to discover the answers for himself, stressing on the 98 percent positivity, empathetically listening, acknowledging by saying thank you, etc.

The practice of coaching is a very tiring process. If, as a coach, you don't feel tired with listening, then probably you have not done enough empathetic listening!

With every coaching session, the coach becomes better at his craft. The benefit is two-way and is highly rewarding for both the trainee and the coach.

The subsequent text elucidates some of the frequently asked questions by the trainees and what Dev had to answer for each of them:

Frequently Asked Questions

Q: What should be a leader's operating style? How much of task orientation and how much of people orientation?

A: It depends. Here the situation leadership model provides the answer. It is different strokes for different folks!

In task orientation, you need to set your goals. In people orientation, there is understanding, empathy and thinking win-win. Task orientation is directive behaviour while people orientation is supportive behavior. Which mix of these two to use depends on the situation or the stage of development of the team member. So, the leader has to diagnose the situation well and prescribe the correct operating style!

Q: What is assertiveness and how to be assertive?

A: To understand assertiveness, one must first understand the causes for non-assertiveness. There are several, but a few important ones are (i) Low self-esteem makes one feel vulnerable (ii) Feeling vulnerable makes one feel threatened (iii) Feeling threatened, one may adopt a two-pronged approach, either becomes aggressive and attacks, or becomes non-assertive and cowers (iv) Both of these lead to stress, which in turn leads to less effective management.

So what is assertiveness? It is an expression of thoughts, feelings and beliefs in open, direct, honest and appropriate ways that do not violate or infringe upon another's rights. It is the ability to act in harmony with your self-esteem without hurting others. Assertiveness implies: (i) Self-awareness (ii) Self-acceptance (iii) Honesty (iv) Empathy (v) Responsibility and (vi) Mutuality.

Examples of assertiveness range from: (i) Refusing requests (ii) Disagreeing and stating your views; agreeing to disagree (iii) Giving criticism and (iv) Receiving criticism.

Q: How to refuse requests?

A: By keeping the reply short and telling the truth. By stating limitations with complete honesty and emphasizing on it. One can refuse requests by asking for clarification and seeking time to consider, by not saying, "I can't", as it sounds like an excuse. And most importantly, by acknowledging the requester.

Q: How to disagree?

A: By disagreeing clearly, expressing doubts in a constructive way, giving reasons for your disagreement, stating the parts of the whole you disagree with and recognizing other people's point of view.

Q: How to give and receive criticism?

A: Give criticism by making sure you are not writing a script in your head, making the criticism specific, explaining as to why you want to raise a topic, asking for a response to your criticism and asking for suggestions to bring about change. Another way for giving criticism is by summarizing the suggestions given and endorsing them.

Receive criticism by asking for clarification if you do not understand; do not take criticism as a personal attack; if a personal attack is made, draw attention to it and ask for a change; if you do not agree, say so impersonally and politely; make sure you agree with suggestions for the future; keep your voice at a normal level; maintain eye contact and do not attack the critic personally.

Q: How to carry out a crucial conversation?

A: In a conversation that veers to angry words or silence, what should one do! How to get unstuck from the seriousness of the situation? The trick is to step out of the content, observe the process and fix it. Work on yourself first, which begins with a change of heart and focusing on what you really want.

Be alert. Learn to look for signs that a conversation is becoming violent and silent. The sooner you catch these signs, the sooner you can return to dialogue and the lesser the damage.

When it comes to crucial conversation, candor does not work; safety does. Learn to step out of the content as staying in the content makes no sense. Steer to safety by recognizing mutual purpose and mutual respect.

How to stay in dialogue when you are angry? It is to recognize that others don't make you mad. It is *you* who makes you mad. Manage your emotions by returning to the source of your feelings. Separate facts from stories. Facts are things that we can see and hear. Stories are judgments and conclusions that can cause us to move to silence and violence.

How to master emotions and return to dialogue? Rethink your story, i.e., your judgment and conclusion. New stories create new feelings and support newer and healthier actions.

How to speak persuasively and not abrasively? Share your path the way you experienced it – from observations to actions. If you start with the facts and are tentative in encouraging others' points of view, you can be both candid and respectful.

How to listen when others blow up? It is your job to make it safe for them to share their facts. Follow a four-step method of asking, mirroring, paraphrasing and priming. Ask to get things rolling. Mirror with the person to understand their feelings. Paraphrase to acknowledge the story. Try coaxing when you are getting nowhere.

How to turn crucial conversations into action and results? There are two steps (1) Deciding on how to decide. Whether by using command, consult, majority vote or consensus (2) Agree on who, what, when, what and follow-up action.

(Source: *Crucial Conversations* by Kerry Patterson, Joseph Grenny, David Maxfield, Ron McMillan and Al Switzler)

Q: How much of anger is too much?

A: Anger should be used sparingly. It should be used as an emergency brake in a limited fashion. Even when you use anger, it should be done with love for the sake of the well-being of the other person as parents do often with their children.

(Source: *Management Mantras* by Sri Sri Ravi Shankar)

Q: How to be completely present in the moment?

A: We are not fully present in the moment when we worry about the future. We are not fully present in the moment when we brood over the past. The answer lies in planning for the future (not worrying) and learning from the past (not brooding). When you are neither planning nor learning (and not worrying or brooding), you are fully in the moment with awareness and alertness. Exercises and practices of deep breathing, yoga and meditation can help one become fully present in the moment.

Q: What is the secret of effective management?

A: It is the secret of holding two seemingly opposites or contrary forces. It is the genius of AND. It is YIN-YANG shown below. It is walking on the razor's edge, like walking on a tightrope. It is understanding the subtlety of being (i) Bold but not a bully (ii) Humble but not apologetic (iii) Confident but not

conceited (iv) Proud but not arrogant (v) Tender but not weak
(vi) Strong but not rude (vii) Firm but not stubborn (viii) Cool
but not cold (ix) In love with life but ready to die (x) Content but
not complacent (xi) Detached but not indifferent (xii) Wise but
not otherwise. Holding the space between dualities (when one
aspect manifests more strongly over the other) is the secret of
effective management.

Yin and Yang depicts the seemingly opposites or contrary
forces that are interconnected and interdependent in the natural
world, and how they give rise to each other as they interrelate
to one another. Many natural dualities (such as light and dark,
high and low, hot and cold, fire and water, life and death, and
so on) are thought of as physical manifestations of the yin-yang
concept.

Yin and yang can be thought of as complementary (instead
of opposing) forces interacting to form a dynamic system in
which the whole is greater than the parts. Everything has both

yin and yang aspects, (for instance, shadow cannot exist without light). Either of the two major aspects may manifest more strongly in a particular object, depending on the criterion of the observation.

Q: How to build confidence and self-esteem?

A: When there is clarity and competence, you build confidence and self-esteem. Chanting mantras (like the *Gayatri Mantra*, *Aditya Hryudayam*, etc.), reading motivational quotes, talking encouraging words and giving auto-suggestions to oneself are the various approaches for building self-confidence.

Q: What did you learn so far on transformation?

A: The flow of the chapters of this book has been my learning on transformation. I have come up with my own mental model

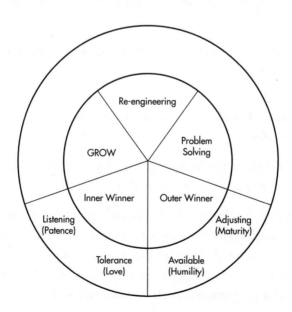

(shown below) that I use frequently when discharging my daily duties at work and at home.

The upper half of the circle (the iceberg visible above the water) covers the four key elements of Re-engineering, GROW, inner winner and outer winner. The lower half of the circle (the iceberg invisible below the water) emphasizes on a character that is based on listening (patience), adjusting (maturity), tolerance (love) and available (humility). The lower half is all about mastery over self. It is an everyday battle over the weaker nature. The more you lead your own self, the easier it becomes to lead others.

On a different note, throughout my career, I reminded myself of an acronym, JASPIH. For me, it meant — never joke, take responsibility and accountability (J), ABC of management, i.e., activate with goals, observe behaviour and deliver consequences, i.e., the one-minute manager (A),take every conversation seriously (S), Brace for problems, objections in every conversation (P), provide immediate clarifications (I) and Help the people you work with (H)

Concentrate on work and not so much on pleasing your employer.

Q: What should be one's approach towards their subordinates?

A: Help them with their growth and development. Create an environment where they can actualize themselves.

Treat their performance appraisals very seriously and fill it up with utmost sincerity. Think of offering the best suggestions possible. Evaluate the appraisal form scientifically: clarify the meaning of the words; clarify the scale; what are the additional items it should contain; general comments/adverse remarks, etc.

Do the appraisals with documentary evidence, never judge hastily, collect enough evidence and only then do it.

Q: What kind of things you should guard against?

A: Guard against emotional instability and ego. Don't take things personally and get affected by people's comments of you not doing well. Avoid wrong company. Avoid wasting time. Beware of setting wrong priorities.

Pursuing excellence in whatever you do should be a way of life!

Q: Would doing an MBA help me?

A: Yes. First let us understand what management of business administration means. One is taught the theory of management and practice. It covers management as a process of getting things done with people working in organized groups. It begins by defining the functions of management and decision-making. It focuses on behaviour sciences, interpersonal relations and leadership. The subject teaches systems thinking, models and processes. Essentially the subject is taught through study and analysis of cases. The general idea is that generalizations can be drawn from cases that can be applied as guides in similar situations.

Management, like medicine, is not an exact science. It is an art and science. Understanding the building blocks of management and business landscape helps one to take better decisions and actions. While success is not 100 percent guaranteed, a good understanding of management surely increases the probability of success. It provides a good guide of what not to do as well as what to do.

Q: Any other way you think that an MBA would help me?

A: Like the law of gravity, all of us are exposed to the ups and downs in life. A deep understanding of management helps one to be on the up most of the time. It also teaches how to bounce back when you are on the down. In other words, a good understanding of management helps one to navigate an upward sustained trajectory with a few occasional downs.

Q: What is the one thing that I should remember after completing my MBA?

A: All the knowledge that you picked up is of no use if you do not apply it. Have the orientation and will to apply the management knowledge.

Post your MBA, continue to read at least four new books on management every year. Also make sure to attend a three-day training program every year on a management topic of your interest and need so that you keep honing your general management skills.

In the course of my professional journey, I found it extremely useful to take the help of Harvard Management Mentor Tools when it came to problem solving and decision-making.

It would further help to go back to a management school after every seven years for a period of three weeks to update oneself on the current thinking and trends in management.

Q: How do you navigate a day?

A: In Chapter 2, the importance of weekly planning has been emphasized. As a day opens up during the week, I revisit the plan for the day by investing 10 minutes. Then, through the day, I focus on being and doing for 10 hours. At the end of the day, I reflect for 20 minutes on the learning from the activities of the day. In other words, I plan, be and learn every day.

This simple method has helped me up my performance and be consistent. It is important to keep striking singles like in the game of cricket every day.

Q: Please tell me more about developing as a leader.

A: This question in answered and elaborated in Chapter 7 and 8. Please read those chapters. If you have come this far in this book, you would have already obtained a good understanding of leadership and how to develop the skill.

Q: Anything that you would like to tell me?

A: Yes. I once met a very successful entrepreneur and invited him for a talk at my business school. He urged the audience to overcome the fear of failure by making a declaration for their future. Citing examples from his childhood, he spoke about the difference in the thinking as an entrepreneur. He said that was the reason behind his success. According to him, an individual has to start thinking from what he wants to be, match that with what he has to do to achieve it and then think about where he is today.

Q: Are there any books on management that have inspired you?

A: There are several. But the *Bhagavad Gita* stands out. The song celestial and its interpretation by several great people had inspired me all along. There are also other books on the *Gita* by Swami Vivekananda, Gandhi and Swami Ranganathanada that are a must read!

Chapters 2 and 3 of the *Bhagavad Gita* are a must read for anyone trying to find meaning in life. According to the *Gita*, the problems we encounter in life are because of the absence of right thinking. What is right thinking? Chapter 2 provides part of the answer. The essence of this chapter is that you are not the body, not the mind and not the intellect. You are the ATMAN, the divine soul. This realization is Jnana Yoga or Sankhya Yoga.

Continuing with the answer for the question 'what is right thinking?' chapter 3 explains the path of action (Karma Yoga). Karma Yoga is about work, proficiency and efficiency. Work is the task to be attended. Proficiency is your knowledge and understanding of the goal, means, ability and self. Efficiency is the application of the proficiency. This way of thinking, which is simple and profound, helps in doing your best.

The essence of chapter 3 is that when you concentrate and focus on the action, the result will take care of itself. Detach from the desire for the result. Do your best (pursue the path of excellence) and leave the rest. Live life keeping others as a reference point. Act with understanding, empathy and love. Surrender your actions to the divine power as an offering. In other words, treat work as worship. Do so with faith, fearlessness and humility. That is right living (Dharma).

In 2008, following the approval from the US Congress, President George W. Bush signed a nuclear deal with India that ended a three-decade ban on the US nuclear trade with Delhi. India successfully launched its first mission to the moon, the unmanned lunar probe Chandrayaan-1. The same year, nearly

200 people were killed and hundreds were injured in a series of coordinated attacks by gunmen in Mumbai. India blamed militants from Pakistan for the attacks and demanded that Islamabad take strong action against those responsible. India announced a "pause" in peace process with Pakistan. The Indian cricket team cancelled their planned tour of Pakistan.

In October 2008, the world economy witnessed a meltdown. While most developed countries witnessed negative growth, India continued to have positive growth, though the rate came down from eight percent to six percent. Barack Obama became the first African-American president of the USA, winning the general election and creating history.

In 2009, resounding general election victory gave governing Congress-led alliance of Prime Minister Dr. Manmohan Singh an enhanced position in parliament, only 11 seats short of an absolute majority.

In 2011, after 34 years of Left Front Government, Trinamool Congress and Congress alliance came to power in West Bengal. That same year, in April, India won the cricket World Cup after almost 28 years (the last win was in 1983 under the captainship of Kapil Dev). This time it was under the able leadership of M.S. Dhoni that India beat Sri Lanka in the finals. India also joined the Trillion Dollar Club in GDP and became the 12th nation in the world to achieve that status.

In 2012, Pranab Mukherjee, the former finance minister was elected the 13th President of India. Ajmal Kasab, the lone surviving gunman of 2008 Mumbai attacks, was hanged in India after a four-year trial. The Golden Quadrilateral road network, connecting the main metros of Delhi, Chennai, Mumbai and Kolkata, was completed. It was one of the most ambitious infrastructure projects of independent India and was started during the NDA government under Vajpayee. In the Olympics that took place in London in August 2012, India garnered eight medals, the highest tally ever, in various sports ranging from boxing, shooting, wresting, etc.

Key Points

To meet challenges, grow and shoulder responsibilities to serve a purpose, it helps to have a coach, a mentor. Alternatively, for you to develop your subordinates, it pays if you can learn the skill of coaching (executive coaching).

Executive coaching is an art and science. It involves the use of the GROW model by the coach while observing the standards of presence. This chapter deals with some of the frequently asked questions that a leader (coach) confronts and the possible answers to subordinates that may help.

The GROW model is a simple, four-step process that will help you structure coaching and mentoring sessions with team members.

You can use the model to help team members improve their performance, and to help them plan for and reach their longer-term career objectives.

FAQ section will provide further insights on management and leadership. It is a MUST read.

This chapter is the fifth step in transforming your life.

Action Points for You

Attend a certification program on executive coaching. There are several. You can pick and choose one where the trainer is certified by the International Coaching Federation (ICF).

CHAPTER | 7

Serving to Grow

A hundred times every day, I remind myself that my inner and outer life depends on the labours of other men, living and dead, and that I must exert myself in order to give in the same measure as I have received and am still receiving.

— Albert Einstein

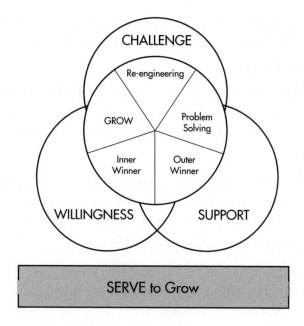

Dev had climbed the ladder in his career with increased responsibilities over a period of time. He started his career as an individual contributor and remained as one for almost five years. Then he got the opportunity for leading a small team. He did not have the benefit of a structured training and coaching program that taught him how to lead at that time. All he had at his disposal was the benefit of readings and observations on the subject of leadership. He learnt the importance of interpersonal relations and he learnt it by trial and error method.

Earlier, Dev's life was simple as an individual contributor as he was responsible only for himself and his work. But now, not only was he responsible for his own work but also accountable for his team's work. This was a big shift for him! Dev asked himself, *Can I start seeing the success of my team members as my success?* He was also aware that not all are comfortable in making this shift.

From small teams, Dev went on to handle larger ones. He realized the importance of structure, responsibility, accountability and goal-setting.

By the time, Dev came into senior levels of management, subjects like strategy, appreciation for other management functions besides one's own functional specialization became crucial.

With respect to human resources skills, coaching or mentoring (discussed in the earlier chapter) and facilitation skills became essential. The more Dev went up the corporate ladder, the more he experienced the need for these skills.

While handling the leadership development efforts for the organization that was a part of his job, Dev read several books on the subject of leadership that included the works of John Kotter, Warren Bennis, Noel Tichy, Ram Charan (*The Leadership Pipeline*), Jim Kouznes, etc.

Most of the works provide the insight that the work of a leader distills down to three important steps. The first task of a leader is to see the future. The second task is alignment, where he aligns the team members to the common goal or purpose. The third task of a leader is motivating his team members.

Dev, in particular, liked the SERVE model of leadership (described by Ken Blanchard). It resonated with the three steps mentioned above and added two more with an emphasis on people and ethics.

S – Seeing the future

E – Enlisting, engaging and empowering the team

R – Re-engineering the processes

V – Valuing people and relationships

E –Embodying Ethics

In his success stories on various key assignments, Dev realized that he in fact had used the five steps in the SERVE model. By putting the first three steps into action, Dev deployed the principles of appreciative inquiry and project management. Most importantly, Dev worked with the objective of making the team win. During those times, Dev kept telling himself: *I may be losing but existence is winning.*

Dev got the opportunity of building a business school from scratch. In the initial days, there were challenges galore. The faculty team was small with only four members. A couple of them left after a short stint feeling uncertain about their future. There was a skeletal administration staff with no accountant and no administration head. Dev worked with his two-member faculty team in coming up with an initial vision document. The document elaborated on the programs that would be designed and launched, the expected number of students who would join, the possible revenue streams and the costs associated and the profitability. In short, Dev primarily worked on the first step of 'seeing the future'.

Then he decided to strengthen the team by recruiting more faculty and non-teaching staff on board. However, the advertisements did not attract too many applicants. Once a new incumbent was selected, Dev paid enough attention to the induction and made sure that the candidate was accepted by the existing team. The candidate was coached on the nature of his work, the goals and his interrelationships with other teammates.

A new employee was closely supervised in the beginning. But as time progressed and the newcomer developed confidence in his tasks, slowly and surely, he was empowered to take decisions on his own. In other words, Dev worked on the second step of 'enlisting, engaging and empowering the team'.

Dev made sure that there were regular weekly meetings. During the meetings, problems related to academics and administration were discussed. With brainstorming and group facilitation, they found solutions to their issues. Alternative solutions were generated and the best one was selected based on cost-benefit analysis. There was an instance where the second batch of working executive students were slated to join but then instructions came from headquarters that unless the first installment was collected there is no way the campus could launch the program. A precedent was set by the first batch in paying the first installment fees almost after two months of the start of their program and the second batch wanted to follow suit. Dev and his team huddled to decide on the best approach. It was decided to give ten days to the prospective students and during this time Dev engaged them on a leadership workshop as a part of their orientation. The plan worked. They paid their fee and the program was launched.

Subsequently, there was another challenge of not enough students enrolling for the management programs. The institute being new faced an uphill task. Dev's team made a promotional video to attract more students. His staff worked hard with focus, determination and exemplary team work. The results were superb and more students joined for classes. In all these instances, Dev was using the third and fourth steps of 're-engineering processes (approach, problem solving, better way of doing, etc.) through people by valuing them'.

All along through his career, Dev kept himself updated by reminding himself: *See into the future (It is the S of the SERVE model). In books, you have certain knowledge of a subject. Make a mental model. While on job, keep updating the information. Update, update, update! Keep track of bestsellers, relevant journals in your related fields. Buy, study, assimilate and implement what is suggested in them.*

High Performance Teams

In different challenging situations, Dev leveraged the team using the principles of appreciative inquiry to carry out a robust dialogue, garner commitment, align the team members towards a common purpose and unleash their energies and talents. A reading of the book *The Wisdom of Teams* by Jon Katzenbach & Douglas Smith provided Dev with a mental model (shown below) that helped him understand what really matters to deliver high performance. In a high-performance team, the members work collectively and experience personal growth. The team members complement each other in their technical skills. They have problem-solving and good interpersonal skills. They work towards specific goals with an agreed approach towards a meaningful purpose. Most important, they demonstrate individual and mutual accountability.

As they progressed with the institute, Dev talked to his team on the importance of project management. In one of the team meetings, Dev said, "As you move ahead in your career, you are likely to face more complex and difficult challenges. Some of these will involve the coordination of many different people, the completion of many tasks in a precise sequence, and the expenditure of a great deal of time and money. Whether you succeed or fail with these projects depends on how good you are at project management."

He encouraged his team to read up on the subject and also visit the website 'Mind Tools' (http://www.mindtools.com/). There are several project management techniques that are covered under the categories of:

- Project Management Framework
- Scheduling
- Scope Management
- Building Support for Your Projects
- Communication
- Change Management
- Project Improvement and Review

Beyond the project management skills, strategic thinking becomes very crucial. The more one steps into senior management levels, the more important it becomes to understand the strategic management framework, models and tools needed to formulate and implement successful business strategies and also understand key learning from successful and unsuccessful cases. Strategy has become a fundamental focal point for organizations. Strategy is the art of working out how you will *win* in business and in life. It is a mix of analysis and intuition. The second element, intuition, grows over the years through the power of observation, contemplation and personal leadership. The first element of analysis has acquired a structured domain of study commonly termed as strategic management. It covers key concepts like

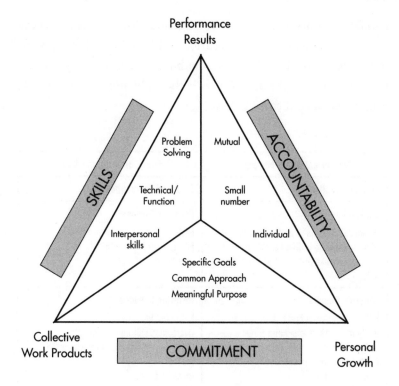

SWOT, Porter's Five Forces, PEST, Competitive Advantage, Core Competence, Blue Ocean Strategy, Mckinsey's 7S Framework, Balanced Scorecard, Execution and Implementation.

Task-People Orientation

Dev learnt that the secret of effective management is holding the space between task and people orientation.

In task orientation, there is clarifying and goal-setting. In people orientation, there is understanding, empathy and thinking win-win. Task orientation is directive behaviour and people orientation is supportive behaviour. Which blend of these two to use depends on the situation or the stage of development of the team member. So, the leader has to diagnose properly and prescribe the operating style with the right mix of task-people orientation as indicated below.

TASK orientation - Manager	PEOPLE orientation - Coach
Setting Direction	**Securing Commitment**
Contracting Organization's plans and priorities and their linkages to individual performance (techniques like Balanced Scorecard can help)	**Creating Purpose** History, context, background Fit between job and talents Clarify and define goals
Securing Results Help the employee break down larger goals into smaller ones and track progress by conducting reviews (techniques like Project Management Approach can help)	**Inspiring to succeed** Help him find own solutions Overcomes self limiting beliefs Confront performance problems with respect Impart job skills (Coaching skills)
Evaluating & Rewarding Confronts performance problems, initiates action and givbes feedback that is fair, honest and just (resolution and assertive skills can be of help)	**Facilitating development** Help develop plan and strategies Track and monitor Challenging work assignments Be a role model Put across employee to network

Trust Building

Whenever the team did not perform, Dev realized that the root cause of the trouble was always low trust. It manifested in no shared vision, misalignment and non-empowerment of the team members. The diagram below picked up from the book *The 8th Habit* by Stephen Covey helped Dev to diagnose the non-performance of teams.

So the solution for a leader lies in building TRUST. One builds trust by keeping promises, respecting another person and not speaking behind the other's back.

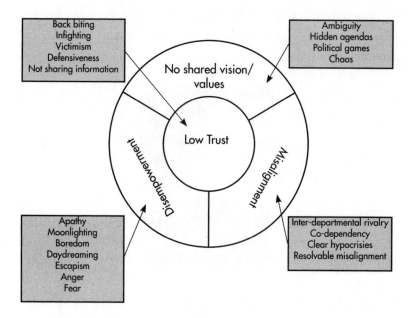

The kind of symptoms of chronic non-performance that one notices in teams are hidden agendas, infighting, ambiguity, apathy, hypocrisy, inter-departmental rivalry, etc. Behind these symptoms are the causes of misalignment, disempowerment and no shared vision. Still further behind these causes is the root cause of LOW TRUST.

So the solution for a leader lies in building TRUST. One builds trust by keeping promises, respecting another person and not speaking behind the other's back.

The essence of successful leadership translates to (i) applying the SERVE Model (ii) Setting an example, walking the talk (iii) Becoming trustworthy and creating a climate of trust.

Around this time, Dev watched the film *Chak De! India*. The movie taught him lessons in leadership and teamwork. In the movie, Kabir Khan (Shah Rukh Khan) becomes the coach for the Indian women's national hockey team and helps them win the World Cup.

Chak De! India is a story about how Kabir Khan (Shah Rukh Khan) coaches and prepares the below-average Indian Women's Hockey Team to become extraordinary by winning the World Cup. The film opens with the Indian team captain Kabir Khan getting a foul in the final minutes of a Hockey World Cup match between Pakistan and India, with Pakistan leading 1-0. Khan chooses to take the penalty stroke himself, but his strike shoots past just above the goal and India loses. Post the match, the media initiates a smear campaign by circulating a photograph of Khan exchanging a handshake with the Pakistani captain, which speculated that Khan, a Muslim, squandered the game to Pakistan's benefit. The religious animosity shown by his neighbours compel Khan and his mother to leave their ancestral home.

Seven years later, Mr. Tripathi (Anjan Srivastav), the head of the India's Hockey Association, meets with hockey advocate Uttamji (Mohit Chauhan) who is Khan's friend. The objective of the meeting was to discuss the Indian women's hockey team. Tripathi has the view that the team has no future. However Uttamji tells him that Khan is ready to coach the team. Though diffident, Tripathi agrees to take the chance in having the Indian women's hockey team coached by Khan.

Khan now finds himself in charge of coaching 16 young women from different parts of India, who lack unity, team spirit and divided by their own prejudices. Komal Chautala (Chitrashi Rawat) from Haryana conflicts with Preeti Sabarwal (Sagarika Ghatge) from Chandigarh. Balbir Kaur (Tanya Abrol) has a short temper and bullies Rani Dispotta (Seema Aazmi) and Soimoi Kerketa (Nisha Nair) who belong to remote places in Jharkhand. Mary Ralte (Kimi Laldawla) from Mizoram and Molly Zimik (Masochon Zimik) from Manipur are treated as foreigners by others. The team's captain Vidya Sharma (Vidya Malvade) is forced to choose between hockey and her husband's family's wishes. Preeti's fiancé Abimanyu Singh (Vivan Bhatena), the vice-captain of the India national cricket team (fictional) feels threatened by her deep involvement with the game.

Khan is tough on the team during the training. To instill the discipline to work as one team, Khan tells his assistant Krishnaji (Vibha Chhibber) to bench the non-complying players including the most experienced player. This leads to Bindia, the experienced player, triggering a revolt that forces Khan to resign. As a farewell gesture, Khan invites Krishnaji, the team manager Sukhlal (Javed Khan) and the girls for lunch. At that time, when a few boys tease Mary, a brawl ensues and the girls beat up the miscreants. This incident brings the girls together and helps cool down their anger towards Khan. On their request to Khan that he remains as a coach, he agrees, impressed by their team spirit and unity.

In a turn of events, Tripathi suddenly decides that the team will not go to Australia for the championship as he feels that they are not fully equipped. Khan throws a challenge to Tripathi that the girls will take on a match with the men's team. Should the girls win, they should be allowed to go to Australia. In the match that follows, the girls lose but earn the praise from the men's hockey team for their courageous and spirited performance. Tripathi changes his mind and sends them to Australia.

During the World Cup, the girls play against Hockeyroos (Australia), Black Sticks Women (New Zealand), Las Leonas (Argentina) and others. Overcoming their individual quest for glory, the girls eventually learn to play as a single unified team with the motto "All for One and One for All". This team bonding leads them to win the championship making their families and country proud. Khan proves his credentials as a winning coach, restores his reputation and demonstrates his loyalty and integrity for the country. He returns along with his mother to his ancestral home, welcome by his once angry neighbours.

Key Lessons

The set of leadership and management lessons are several. Here are five lessons that are distilled.

Lesson 1: Making Impossible Possible

In the movie, Kabir Khan makes the seemingly impossible goal of winning the Women's World Cup in hockey possible. Khan trains the team to overcome their preconceived notions on the challenge, makes them believe in their capabilities, makes them work hard and think smart to achieve the audacious goal.

> In our lives, too, we face tough challenges. We need to believe in ourselves, have a vision and work hard and smart to overcome the challenges.

Lesson 2: Teamwork

In the beginning, neither the players nor the authorities were sure of winning the game but Kabir Khan motivated them to work as one team and win. He drilled the message in each team member that she is an Indian player first and a regional player second. He constantly reminded them that first, one is playing for the country, then the team and if any strength is left, then for oneself. He stimulated team spirit and developed the "We" feeling towards a common purpose of winning the World Cup. He developed the enthusiasm in the players to win not as an individual but as a team.

> Teamwork is essential for achieving insurmountable goals. Breaking norms, personal egos, complacency and aligning the team with the goal is crucial.

Lesson 3: Leadership Style

In the beginning, Kabir Khan was tough by reprimanding, firing and suspending the players who were not following the instructions. Later he provides motivation by encouraging them, helping them to overcome their weaknesses, focuses on their development and gains acceptance.

> A true leader works hand in hand with his subordinates unlike a boss who orders.

Lesson 4:   Seeing Challenges as Opportunities

In the movie, Kabir Khan, an ex-hockey captain with a blemished image, was selected as the coach since the board had no faith in the women's hockey team to do any better. He takes up the challenge as an opportunity to answer his critics and guides the women's hockey team to victory.

> Opportunities come disguised as challenges. The next time you are faced with a challenge, you know what to do!

Lesson 5:   Staying Focused and Committed

In his pursuit of winning the World Cup, Kabir Khan faces many obstacles.

In the film, the team faces rough play by the Argentinian team. He comes up with a winning strategy by personally meeting, notwithstanding their earlier altercation, and motivating the experienced Bindia Naik who knows how to play against them.

Through will power, focus and commitment, he endeavors in keeping the team knitted, committed to reach the goal.

> Firm resolve and determination will help one to overcome all odds.

The essence of successful leadership translates to (i)
applying the SERVE Model (ii) Setting an example,
walking the talk (iii) Becoming trustworthy and creating a
climate of trust.

The Choice is Yours

During his younger days, Dev had a penchant for attending
spiritual discourses. With time, he felt less need to attend them.
Once, instead of attending such a lecture, he went to buy a
smartphone that had been long pending in his list of things to do.
He started giving more and more importance to practice than the
mere act of attending the talks. The universal truths are simple.
It is all about practicing those truths daily, like Vivekananda said
that he valued playing football more than the mere act of talking.
It is more important to be an actor on stage than be a part of the
audience in the balcony. There is guts and glory in the act rather
than in watching and sermonizing.

Every day, one has a choice to lead an ordinary life or a powerful
life. The choice is YOURS!

The day you lead an ordinary life, you experience a victimized
mind and an indulgent body. You are a social mirror for others.
You do not live the day on your terms.

Every day, one has a choice to lead an ordinary life or a
powerful life. The choice is YOURS!

The day you lead a powerful life, you experience a visionary mind, a disciplined body and a passionate heart. You live the day on your terms.

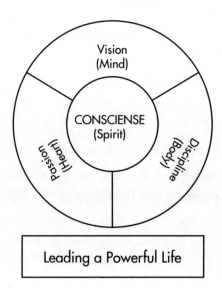

The essence of leading a powerful life is beautifully captured in the Buddhist saying that reads as follows:

"Where vision is 1 year, cultivate flowers

Where vision is 10 years, cultivate trees

Where vision is 100 years, cultivate people."

In leading a powerful life, your paradigm should be, "I may be losing but existence is winning." You are unselfish and you tell yourself that which is unselfish is moral and all the others are immoral.

One day, Dev reflected on his journey so far and could see how he had moved from security needs to affiliation and recognition needs on the pyramid of Maslow's Hierarchy of Needs. He felt that most of the time he was operating in the zone beyond the recognition and esteem needs, towards self-realization at the top.

As life unfolded in 2013, Dev's son completed his MBBS and wanted to pursue higher studies abroad.

It has been a tumultuous period for India and the world from 2008 onwards, following the global financial crisis.

In 2010, the Common Wealth Games scam put India in a fix. In March 2011, the 2G scam rocked the country. Anti-corruption activist Anna Hazare went on a fast on April 5, 2011, to bring a strong Jan Lokpal bill in the country to alleviate corruption.

Arvind Kejriwal, who had started his NGO Parivarthan in 1998, realized his NGO's impact was limited. He felt that there was a need to change the way politicians operated in the country. Along with Hazare, Kejriwal started the Jan Lokpal movement.

Their protest against graft was successful as support poured in from all walks of life. The movement gathered further momentum when Hazare went on a fast in August 2011. Anna succeeded to get the government to discuss the passing of the bill as per certain predefined timelines. The bill passed through the Lok Sabha. The nation waited with anticipation to see if it would get cleared by the Rajya Sabha in December, praying and hoping that a new dawn would be ushered into the country from the New Year. But that was not destined to happen. The bill did not get passed with all the amendments sought by the social activists of the anti-graft movement.

The effort continued with Anna and India Against Corruption (IAC) following with the agitation in August 2012. But support for the movement dwindled. A difference of opinion within IAC emerged, with Anna Hazare opting for sustaining the movement non-politically while Kejriwal wanting to continue the fight politically. On Gandhi's birthday, Kejriwal announced a new political party, Aam Aadmi Party (AAP).

There has been no respite on the anti-graft movement since then. Starting with the Commonwealth Games scam, then the 2G scam, and finally the Coalgate scam, the nation had witnessed corruption like never before. The citizens of this country had been witnessing bold actions from the Comptroller and Auditor General and a few IAS officers like Ashok Khemka when they passed orders for an inquiry of Robert Vadra's (Congress president Sonia Gandhi's son-in-law) DLF land deals. The nation is going through a churn. Like in the mythological story, the poison in the system is slowly coming out, leaving the room for nectar to emerge.

In November 2013, the country honoured legendary cricketer Sachin Tendulkar with a Bharat Ratna on his retirement from cricket.

In 2013, the Indian Space Research Organisation (ISRO) successfully launched Mars Orbiter Mission. The year ended with the Aam Aadmi Party's Arvind Kejriwal becoming the chief minister of Delhi. But most importantly, the Jan Lokpal Bill was passed after over three years.

In 2014, a resounding general election victory paved way for the NDA-led alliance of BJP to come to power and gave a chance to Prime Minister Narendra Modi to redefine the future of India.

India is now standing at a threshold where if it grows at above eight percent, it will overtake the GDPs of countries like UK, France and Germany from 2016 onwards, over a period of eight years. In fact, India overtook UK in GDP towards the end of 2016 by becoming the sixth largest economy. By 2030, India is likely to reach the third rank in terms of GDP, trailing US and China.

India certainly has the potential to do this and could probably do it faster with better governance. Should all the black money get into the accounted stream, the growth rate of this country would be two percentage points higher than the current reported growth rate. As a nation, the common man prays that integrity and cleanliness comes into systems, so that poverty alleviation takes place much faster and India finds its rightful place in the global arena more quickly.

What we are now witnessing is history in the making.

Key Points

In this chapter, emphasis is given on the SERVE model of leadership.

In leadership teams, it is useful to note that teams that deliver high performance are those teams where the members work collectively, experience personal growth, complement each other in their technical and problem-solving skills, demonstrate individual and mutual accountability, and most importantly, have a common approach with a meaningful purpose.

While leading teams, it is useful to have a heightened awareness on the task-people orientation and also understand that behind the symptoms of chronic problems, the root cause is always less trust.

Lastly, the chapter triggers one to make a choice of leading a powerful life with a visionary mind, a disciplined body and a passionate heart.

This chapter is the sixth step in transforming your life.

Action Points for You

1. Learning to apply the SERVE model of leadership.

2. Understanding the elements of high performance teams.

3. Holding the space between task and people orientation.

4. Understanding that behind the symptoms of chronic problems is always the issue of low trust.

5. Making a choice every day between leading a powerful life vis-à-vis an ordinary life.

CHAPTER | **8**

Wrap Up

I shall be telling this with a sigh

Somewhere ages and ages hence:

Two roads diverged in a wood, and I----

I took the one less traveled by,

And that has made all the difference

– Robert Frost

Leadership and strategy are inseparable. There is an intimate ongoing connection between the two. Strategy is not a problem to be solved and settled. Good strategies are never signed, sealed and delivered. There will be aspects of the plan that need to be clarified, several unexpected contingencies to be dealt with. It's a journey and requires continuous leadership.

The leader must oversee this ongoing process. Time and again, he must observe, identify, weigh, decide and act. He must pursue certain opportunities and decline the others. He bears the responsibility for setting a firm's direction and make decisive choices day after day. It is a difficult role and requires a level of courage. A leader should be able to live with the difficult question, *what I do today, will it matter tomorrow?* The little you do today is likely to matter more.

The old-fashioned view of leadership is that leaders are marked out for leadership from early on in their lives; and that if you are not a born leader, there is little you can do to become one. That is not the way management thinkers see it now. The modern view is that through patience, persistence and hard work, you can be a truly effective leader, just as long as you make the effort needed for serving to grow and growing to serve.

The diagram below captures the learning of all the previous chapters; starting with the fundamental paradigm of leadership development through challenge-willingness-support, followed by the concept of inner winner-outer winner within the context of growing to serve and serving to grow in a 360-degree way, with responsibilities towards subordinates, peers, boss and family.

Today Dev has a sense of gratitude towards people who he had known and worked closely with. He feels indebted to his mentors who made a difference in his life; there were five of them at different stages of his career and life. The one person, who had been his mentor, his role model throughout his life thus far, had been his father.

When Dev was in primary school, he once broke a glass tabletop during a fight with his cousin. Dev ran away from home, but with great timidity returned in the evening during teatime, expecting to get an earful from his father. Instead, his father smiled at him and said that he was happy that Dev did not get hurt during the melee. He explained that the broken glass was not a problem as he can easily replace it. That lesson left an indelible impression on young Dev's mind: attack the problem and not the person.

Once his father returned home from the hospital by a cycle-rickshaw as the car had gone for repairs. He gave the rickshaw puller the negotiated Rs 1.50 and as the man was leaving, Dev's father stopped and tipped him 50 paisa more. The rickshaw puller was delighted because that was his asking price. Dev's father deliberately negotiated the price down but invariably gave the other party what they had asked for. These were the little ways of his father that made Dev feel proud to be his son.

Dev's father was Robin Hood in the eyes of his poor patients. He never charged them any fee for his treatments. But from the ones that could afford it, he took his rightful fees. He was a terrific doctor and had a roaring practice. Later, after retirement, when he shifted to his new home, his old clientele continued to visit him.

BOSS

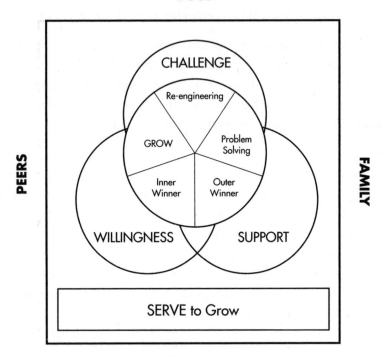

SUBORDINATES

What amazes Dev even today is that not only did his father take care of his wife and children but also looked after his younger siblings and others in the family and provided them with platforms to launch themselves in their respective careers. Today Dev's uncles look up to Dev's parents as foster parents and that is hugely endearing. Dev's father's discipline and hard work and his mother's patience and nurturing created a great home, a sweet home, for many!

In 2010, Dev's father, who by then was in his eighties, had to undergo a surgery. Post the surgery, his health recouped but later deteriorated. Today Dev's father stays confined to his room and bed, hardly talking, but instead speaking with his eyes. Dev sees divinity in his mother in the way she takes care of his father. Dev's parents make a great couple, trusting and supporting one another for the last 65 years of their married life. Through their lives, they have set a great example for their children to emulate. Between them, they orchestrated and provided the right strokes to their children to make them come up in the battle of life. Dev, his brothers and sister are mightily proud of their parents for what they have done for them and how little they have asked from them in return.

In Chapter 2, we discussed how Dev, in his thirties, arrived at certain values for himself: Career Growth, Discipline, Integrity, Relationships, Wealth and Personal Development.

Over time, Dev kept reading and learning, and now he has reached his fifties. Further readings of the *Mahabharata* by various writers like Kamala Subramaniam, Gurcharan Das (*The Difficulty of Being Good*), Devdutt Pattanaik (*Jaya*) helped Dev to develop a deeper understanding of those values.

There is no better way to understand what matters most than through anecdotes and stories in the *Mahabharata*. During their exile, the Pandavas stopped somewhere to rest. To quench their thirst, Yudhishtir sent his brothers one after the other to fetch water. All the brothers came across a lake separately that was guarded by a *yaksha* (a spirit that guards the natural resources). The yaksha demands them to answer his questions before taking water from the lake. None of them paid any heed and tried to drink from the lake before answering the *yaksha*. As a result, they fell dead one by one on the bank of the lake. A worried Yudhishtir came to search for his brothers and found their dead bodies. The yaksha repeats the demand to the elder Pandava too. This time Yudhishtir asnwered the *yaksha's* questions correctly. This pleased the *yaksha* so much so that he gave his brothers' lives back as a gift to Yudhishtir.

The *yaksha's* questions helped Dev to appreciate the meaning of values further. A few of them are emphasized below.

Q: What is more valuable than gold?

A: Knowledge

Q: More desirable than wealth?

A: Health

So Dev noted that it is health, knowledge and wealth!

Q: What measures a man?

A: Conduct

Q: What is the greatest deed?

A: Non-violence

Dev thought that perhaps Gandhi found his answer on non-violence as the means to achieve the end, i.e., freedom for India, here in the *yaksha's* question.

Q: What is simplicity?

A: Equanimity

Q: What is the only thing man can conquer?

A: His own mind

The story of the Mahabharata ends not with the victory of the Pandavas over the Kauravas but with Yudhishtira's conquest over himself. This is the spiritual victory or *JAYA*. This is the ultimate message of the great epic.

Q: What when renounced makes one wealthy?

A: Desire

Q: What when renounced makes one agreeable?

A: Pride

Q: What is the worst disease?

A: Greed

Q: Who is man's most dreaded enemy?

A: Anger

Q: Most desired form of happiness?

A: Contentment

Dev realized that the message of the *Gayatri Mantra* embodies the expulsion of impurities like the ones mentioned above, i.e., greed, anger, pride and infusion of purities like contentment, equanimity, etc.

Q: How does one know the true path?

A: Not through arguments – they never reach a conclusion; not from teachers – they can only give opinions; to know the true path one must, in silence and solitude, reflect on one's own life.

Q: What is the most amazing thing about the world?

A: Everyday people die, yet the rest live as if they are immortal.

In the final part of the *Mahabharata*, as Yudhishtir steps into heaven, *swarg*, he sees the Kauravas there. The gods, *devas*, tell him that as they died in the holy place of Kurukshetra, the Kauravas got the merit to come to heaven despite their demerits before the Kurukshetra war. But Yudhishtir could not find his brothers in heaven and when asked about their whereabouts, the gods lead him to a dark forsaken place. It is in this misery, *narak*, Yudhishtir finds his brothers and wife, Draupadi. The gods, *devas,* tell Yudhishtir that Bhima was paying for gluttony, Arjuna for envy, Nakula for insensitivity, Sahadeva for smugness and Draupadi for partiality. The gods tell Yudhishtir to return to *swarg* without them. But Yudhishtir refuses to get back to heaven because his attachment and loyalty was with his brothers and wife. The gods taunt him to rise above his attachments to his kith and kin as in heaven one is expected to do so.

Yudhishtir still refuses to budge as he is unable to understand why the Kauravas could have the doors of heaven open for them. The gods then remind Yudhishtir that even after the war and thirty-six years of rule over Hastinapur, he has not overcome his hatred for the Kauravas. It was at this stage, Yudhishtir experienced a WOW moment! He realized that he has not yet overcome his prejudices. He then determined to forgive the Kauravas. There was no more hatred. No more "them" and "us". No more better and worse. There was only love. Everyone was one. Yudhishtir had won the ultimate victory, the victory over himself! Now Yudhishtir could ascend to *Vaikunta*, an abode higher than heaven.

Dev also felt that the 4Ls mentioned by Stephen Covey can constitute the platform for one's values. The 4 Ls are Learn, Live, Love and Legacy. When you learn, you grow and serve. When you serve (think more of others and less of self), you live. By learning and living, you grow to serve and serve to grow. And in this existence of learning and living, if you love everyone, then you will leave a lasting contribution, a whiff of fragrance, a LEGACY!

Every now and then, Dev used to remind himself — *Strive for excellence, the act itself gives tremendous joy. It is like realizing God. This striving despite its non-perfection, if done as worship to God, will give great peace and happiness. You would not get depressed by your failing. Instead ask yourself why you could not perform better. Reason out as to why you had not done as well as you should have. At the same time, you should not become overjoyed and complacent after your success.*

For Dev, the quintessence of the *Bhagavad Gita* was i) Do your allotted work sincerely ii) Renounce the fruits of your work iii) Love everyone iv) Surrender to Him with full trust.

A young MBA student once asked Dev, the Dean, the following question.

What is God according to you?

Dev replied: *Sat Chit Ananda*

The student did not understand.

Dev said that it is Truth, Mindfulness and Happiness or Bliss

The student clarified that by experiencing this state, is he terming it as God.

Dev said yes. Elaborating further, he said that an action that leads to this state is experiencing God. Invariably when one pursues actions that are excellent, one attains this state.

The student then asked does it mean then when one has not attained a gold standard in excellent action, one cannot term that one is experiencing God.

For which Dev replied that as long as you do better than yesterday, you are attaining God. It is a journey and therefore not an end to the gold standard.

Then the student asked what if one feels happy pursuing materialistic pleasures.

To which Dev replied that such pursuits give temporary pleasure but not true happiness or bliss that sticks when you pursue actions that are outward looking, not self-centred and excellent.

After his return from South Africa to India, Gandhi set up Sabarmati Ashram where he lived, worked and wrote. Once an inmate of the ashram asked Gandhi how was he going to help India get independence if he just sat there spinning his *charka*. Gandhi said that he himself did not know how. But he had faith that it was the right thing to do if we have to get independence.

So to answer the question by the student, whether operating the management tools would help one make a difference, the answer is that to have faith and belief in the management tools. Keep using them like turning the spinning wheel. The momentum will pick up and one day you will achieve your goal.

Dev developed an attitude for gratitude. He constantly told himself not to forget to be grateful to all those who made a difference to him so far in his life. As someone said, "Gratitude is one of the sweet short-cuts to finding peace of mind and happiness inside. No matter what is going on outside of us, there is always something we could be grateful for."

Dev was thankful to God for giving him those flashes of insight that made him take the road less travelled. Quoting Robert Frost, Dev told himself: *Two roads diverged in a wood and I took the one less travelled by, and that has made all the difference.*

ACTION POINTS - SUMMARY

CH. NO.	CHAPTER TITLE	ACTION POINTS
1	Challenges	1. Drawing your life's journey like in the second diagram of the chapter. It is immaterial how old you are. Draw it from school days till now. 2. Do you see the ups and downs? You do not need to be an expert to figure out the answers behind the ups and downs. Be candid and truthful with yourself. 3. Now at this point of time in your life, draw the 360 degree profile as noted in the last diagram of this chapter. 4. For each of the relationships in the 360, come up with plans to nurture them! 5. Last but not the least, do not forget to take good care of yourself.
2	Inner Winner (First step in transforming your life)	1. Begin with planning for the week. Please note that it is not planning for the day but planning for the week. It takes around 45 minutes to do it by sitting in a quiet corner on a Sunday morning, maybe. It seems easy but it is difficult to practice. Practice it for four weeks and you will experience a big change. 2. Reflecting and meditating upon writing down your statement of purpose or your mission statement. It will give direction to your roles and goals. 3. Taking time to ponder over what you value in life. The values will help guide your daily decision making. 4. Reading the books listed in the table in the appendix so as to develop a winner's mindset. Some of the suggested books are (i) *Think and Grow Rich* (ii) *The Power of Positive Thinking*. 5. Reading biographies/autobiographies of people whom you admire and see as role models.

| 3 | Outer Winner (Second step in transforming your life) | 1. Practicing empathy. Making an effort to understand the other person's perspectives and feelings.
2. Honing social skills that involve communication, influence and resolving conflicts.
3. Becoming a one-minute manager with goal setting, praise and reprimand.
4. Building trust. At the root of it is learning to keep promises and genuinely respecting another individual.
5. Thinking win-win. Creative problem solving and coming up with a third alternative so that you win and the other person wins, too.
6. Practicing abundance.
7. Remembering that all the above points are work in progress and there is no end to perfection.
8. Reading biographies/autobiographies of people whom you admire and see as role models.
9. Seeing films listed in the appendix from a management perspective of leadership and team work. |
| 4 | Problem Solving (Third step in transforming your life) | 1. Practice the 7-step problem solving method. |

5	Reengineering Yourself (Fourth step in transforming your life)	1. Learning to apply situational leadership. 2. Leveraging group's diversity and creating group synergy. 3. Reading the books listed in the appendix. Making summary points and reducing it to a mnemonic. Applying the learning. 4. Seeing films listed in the appendix from a management perspective of leadership and team work. 5. Making it a point to listen to the interviews of celebrities, successful business men, etc.
6	Growing to serve (Fifth step in transforming your life)	1. Attend a certification program on executive coaching. There are several. You can pick and choose one where the trainer is certified by the International Coaching Federation (ICF).
7	Serving to grow (Sixth step in transforming your life)	1. Learning to apply the SERVE model of Leadership. 2. Understanding the elements of high performance teams. 3. Holding the space between task-people orientation. 4. Behind the symptoms of chronic problems is the root cause of low trust. 5. Making a choice every day between leading a powerful life vis-à-vis an ordinary life
8	Wrap-up	1. The mental model of the diagram that captures the learning of all the previous chapters. 2. Value clarification at times of dilemmas.

Annexures

List of books that shaped Dev's thinking and how he applied the learning through mnemonics.

DEV'S AGE	BOOK	AUTHOR	IMPACT
Formative, from 8-12 years	*Amar Chitra Katha*, The *Mahabharata*, The *Ramayana* (Rajagopalachari), *Krishnavathara* (KM Munshi), *Phantom*, *Tarzan* (Edgar Rice Burroughs) and other classics.		Taught to be heroic.
During Teenage	Encyclopedia Britannica, *The Adventures of Sherlock Holmes* by Arthur Conan Doyle, Agatha Christie's books		Taught to be scientific and analytical.
	Swami Vivekananda Quotes	Ramakrishna Math	Taught to have high self-esteem, application; double promotion and taking time progressively to come first in the class; high influence of his father.
	The Power of Positive Thinking	Dale Carnegie	Taught positive thinking.

	Think and Grow Rich	Napoleon Hill	Taught about using affirmations.
	Jonathan Livingstone Seagull	Richard Bach	Taught about lifelong learning; building skills and reaching new worlds.
Twenties	*The One-Minute Manager*	Spencer Johnson & Ken Blanchard	Helped to build his Emotional Quotient (EQ).
	One Minute for Myself	Spencer Johnson	Taught about finding a balance.
	The Godfather	Mario Puzzo	Learning for business.
Thirties	*The 7 Habits of Highly Effective People*	Stephen Covey	Taught to make sense of the uncertainties in situations and people and come up with an action plan for self.
	Situational Leadership	Ken Blanchard	Helped Dev in teaching cycling to his son and subsequently to deliver the right styles to get the work done.
	Building High Performance Teams	Ken Blanchard	Taught about leading teams.
	The Goal	Eliyahu Goldratt	Taught about enhancing efficiency.
	Oh, Mind Relax Please	Swami Sukhabodhananda	Values
	The Road Less Travelled	Scott Peck	Discipline and love.
Forties	*Good to Great*	Jim Collins	Level 5 leadership
	You Can Win	Shiv Khera	Attitude, focus, inspirational stories.
	The Fifth Discipline	Peter Senge	Mental models, systems thinking, personal mastery.

	Wings of Fire	Dr. A.P.J. Abdul Kalam	Integrity, responsibility, service.
	The Alchemist	Paulo Coelho	Dream, ambition.
	The Monk Who Sold His Ferrari	Robin Sharma	Character development, discipline.
	The Leader Who Had No Title	Robin Sharma	Leadership at any position.
	The Art of Living	Sri Sri Ravi Shankar	Taught about *Sudarshan Kriya.*
	Crucial Conversations	Kerry Patterson, Joseph Grenny, David Maxfield, Ron McMillan & Al Switzler	Tools for talking when stakes are high, opinions vary and emotions run strong.
	The Power of Intention	Wayne Dyer	Changed the way he looked at things.
Fifties	*The Difficulty of Being Good*	Gurcharan Das	Values, principles, a guide for dilemma resolution.
	Jaya	Devdutt Pattanaik	Retelling of the *Mahabharata.*
	Great by Choice	Jim Collins	Discipline, creativity and contingency planning.
	Vivekachudamani	Swami Ranganathananda	Wisdom of the Vedas as interpreted by Sri Sankaracharya.

A list of training Dev attended that shaped his thinking and practice:

DEV'S AGE	TRAINING	FACILITATOR	IMPACT
Teens	Talks on the *Gita*	Great discourses by the monks at the Ramakrishna Math.	Possibly helped him achieve academic excellence and become a good student.
Continuous	Mentoring	Dev's father	One liners from the *Gita*, other books, etc.
Thirties	LIFE Program	Swami Sukhabodhananda	Helped him learn values from Indian ethos.
Forties	Senior Leadership Training	Clive Rubery	Helped him build an NGO related to leadership development of doctors, nurses and paramedics.
	Landmark Forum	Mahesh (a faculty)	Helped him to carry out crucial conversations.
	AOL Satsangs	Sri Sri Ravi Shankar	Helped him with conversations and dialogue.
	Executive Coaching	Peter Reding, Coach for Life	Helped him transform an NGO in health care delivery.

A list of movies that shaped Dev's thinking and practice:

DEV'S AGE	FILMS	DIRECTOR	LESSONS
Leadership			
Teens	*The Magnificent Seven*	John Sturges	Leadership & teamwork
	The Ten Commandments	Cecil B. DeMille	Leadership
	The Guns of Navarone	Joseph Logan Thompson, Alexander Mackendrick	Leadership & teamwork
	Where Eagles Dare	Brian G. Hutton	Teamwork
	Sholay	Ramesh Sippy	Friendship
Twenties	*Gandhi*	Richard Attenborough	Leadership
	The Godfather	Francis Ford Coppola	Leadership
	The Untouchables	Brian De Palma	Leadership & teamwork
	Mahabharat (TV show)	B.R. Chopra	Values, principles, leadership
Thirties	*Lawrence of Arabia*	David Lean	Leadership
	Genghis Khan	Henry Levin	Leadership
Forties	*Gladiator*	Ridley Scott	Leadership
	Lagaan	Ashutosh Gowarikar	Leadership & teamwork
	The Passion of the Christ	Mel Gibson	Leadership
	Swades	Ashutosh Gowarikar	Leadership

	Chak De! India	Shimit Amin	Leadership &teamwork
	Iqbal	Nagesh Kukunoor	Coaching & leadership
	The Legend of Bagger Vance	Robert Redford	Coaching &leadership
	The Karate Kid	John G. Avildsen	Coaching
	Avatar	James Cameron	Leadership
Inspirational Courage			
Teens	*Ben-Hur*	William Wyler	Triumph
	The Great Escape	John Sturges	The human spirit
Twenties	*Papillon*	Franklin J. Schaffner	Never-say-die attitude
Thirties	*First Blood*	Ted Kotcheff	Never-say-die attitude
	Cliffhanger	Renny Harlin	Never-say-die attitude
	Speed	Jan De Bont	Never-say-die attitude
	The Bourne Identity	Doug Liman	Never-say-die attitude
Forties	*Cast Away*	Robert Zemeckis	Never-say-die attitude
	The Pursuit of Happyness	Gabriele Muccino	Persistence
	Predator	John McTiernan	Never-say-die attitude
	Behind the Enemy Lines	John Moore	Never-say-die attitude
Fifties	*Gravity*	Alfonso Cuarón	Never-say-die attitude

Selected Bibliography

Emotional Intelligence by Daniel Goleman

The 7Habits of Highly Effective People by Stephen Covey

8th Habit by Stephen Covey

The One-Minute Manager by Dr. Spencer Johnson

Situational Leadership by Kenneth Blanchard

The Road Less Travelled by Scott Peck

Crucial Conversations by Kerry Patterson, Joseph Grenny, David Maxfield, Ron McMillan, and Al Switzler

The Wisdom of Teams by John Katzenbach

What the CEO Really Wants from You by R.Gopalakrishnan

Oh, Mind Relax Please by Swami Sukhabodhananda

Management Mantras by Sri Sri Ravi Shankar

Jaya by Devdutt Pattanaik

Vivekachudamani by Swami Ranganathananda

The Difficulty of Being Good by Gurcharan Das

Wikipedia

Acknowledgements

So far in my life I've had several teachers and mentors. My late father, Dr. Ramalingam, was my first teacher and mentor and always remained so ever since. He has taught me more than I could ever give him credit for. He has been an excellent role model for everyone in the family and our community at large. He was an exemplary doctor and human being.

Nobody has been more important to me in the pursuit of this project than my family. I would like to thank my mother, Mrs. Rukmini Ramalingam, whose love and guidance are with me in whatever I pursue. Most importantly, I wish to thank my loving and supportive wife, Vedavani; my sister Dr. Uma; my two elder brothers, Dr. Prabhakar and Mr. Sudhakar; and also to my extended family who have always provided me with unlimited motivation.

Last but not the least, this book would not have been possible without the support of Ms. Sandhya Iyer (Managing Editor), Mr. Akash Shah (Publisher) at Jaico Publishing House and their entire editorial team. My heartfelt gratitude to all those who have worked with me in the making of this book.

JAICO PUBLISHING HOUSE
Elevate Your Life. Transform Your World.

ESTABLISHED IN 1946, Jaico Publishing House is home to world-transforming authors such as Sri Sri Paramahansa Yogananda, Osho, The Dalai Lama, Sri Sri Ravi Shankar, Sadhguru, Robin Sharma, Deepak Chopra, Jack Canfield, Eknath Easwaran, Devdutt Pattanaik, Khushwant Singh, John Maxwell, Brian Tracy and Stephen Hawking.

Our late founder Mr. Jaman Shah first established Jaico as a book distribution company. Sensing that independence was around the corner, he aptly named his company Jaico ('Jai' means victory in Hindi). In order to service the significant demand for affordable books in a developing nation, Mr. Shah initiated Jaico's own publications. Jaico was India's first publisher of paperback books in the English language.

While self-help, religion and philosophy, mind/body/spirit, and business titles form the cornerstone of our non-fiction list, we publish an exciting range of travel, current affairs, biography, and popular science books as well. Our renewed focus on popular fiction is evident in our new titles by a host of fresh young talent from India and abroad. Jaico's recently established Translations Division translates selected English content into nine regional languages.

Jaico's Higher Education Division (HED) is recognized for its student-friendly textbooks in Business Management and Engineering which are in use countrywide.

In addition to being a publisher and distributor of its own titles, Jaico is a major national distributor of books of leading international and Indian publishers. With its headquarters in Mumbai, Jaico has branches and sales offices in Ahmedabad, Bangalore, Bhopal, Bhubaneswar, Chennai, Delhi, Hyderabad, Kolkata and Lucknow.

SINCE 1946